D1349295

The Complete
Family Cookbook

Published in 2010 by ACP Books, Sydney
ACP Books are published by ACP Magazines
a division of PBL Media Pty Limited

Published by ACP Books, a division of
ACP Magazines Ltd, 54 Park St, Sydney;
GPO Box 4088, Sydney, NSW 2001.
Telephone (02) 9282 8618; fax (02) 9267 9438.
acpbooks@acpmagazines.com.au;
www.acpbooks.com.au
Printed and bound in China
United Kingdom Distributed by Australian Consolidated
Press (UK),
Telephone (01604) 642 200; fax (01604) 642 300;
books@acpuk.com

A catalogue record for this book is available from the
British Library
ISBN 978-1-903777-91-6
© ACP Magazines Ltd 2010
ABN 18 053 273 546
This publication is copyright. No part of it may be
reproduced or transmitted in any form without the written
permission of the publishers.

Special features and chapter openers:
Photographers Maree Homer, Louise Lister
Stylists Louise Bickle, Kate Nixon

The publishers would like to thank the following for props
used in photography: The Bay Tree, Woollahra; Prop Stop,
St Peters; Victoria's Basement, Alexandria; No Chintz,
Woollahra; Chef's Warehouse, Surry Hills; Rhubarb, Richmond
(Vic); Vicino, Waterloo; ici et la, Surry Hills; Butterfield Tate
Gallery, Waterloo.

Scanpan cookware is used in the AWW Test Kitchen.

To order books
Telephone: 01604 642 200
Order online: www.acpuk.com

THE AUSTRALIAN Women's Weekly

The Complete Family Cookbook

acp books

contents

bringing families

Our lives have changed a lot over the past few decades. We're busier and more stressed than ever before, so it's easy to see how the family meal has fallen by the wayside. With both parents often working long hours and juggling kids' music, sporting and social commitments, it can be tough to get the whole family together for a meal. It's all too easy when everyone is hungry and tired at the end of the day to eat at different times or to collapse in front of the television balancing a plate on your lap. But eating together is an important part of family life. Mealtimes provide the perfect opportunity for families to bond and connect with each other. It's a chance to share what's going on in our lives, talk about what happened in our day and to discuss the news and current affairs. Mealtimes should be an exchange of ideas, conversation and feelings. They are a unifying experience for the family, fostering warmth, love and a sense of belonging. Eating family meals together is also associated with eating more healthfully. Home-cooked meals are usually far more nutritious and healthy than takeaway alternatives. They tend to contain more fruits and vegetables and essential nutrients that are vital to our health and wellbeing. Cooking and serving meals at home also means you have more control over the

If you like canned baked beans then just wait till you taste these homemade ones. It takes a little more time, but is well worth it.

breakfast beans on toast

2 cups (400g) dried cannellini beans
1 tablespoon olive oil
1 large brown onion (200g), chopped coarsely
2 cloves garlic, sliced thinly
2 rindless bacon rashers (130g), chopped coarsely
2 tablespoons brown sugar
¼ cup (60ml) maple syrup
1 tablespoon dijon mustard
400g can chopped tomatoes
1 litre (4 cups) water
6 x 1cm-thick slices sourdough bread
2 tablespoons coarsely chopped
  fresh flat-leaf parsley

1 Place beans in large bowl, cover with water; stand overnight, drain. Rinse under cold water, drain.
2 Heat oil in large saucepan, add onion, garlic and bacon; cook, stirring, until onion softens. Stir in beans, sugar, syrup and mustard. Add undrained tomatoes and the water; bring to the boil. Reduce heat; simmer, covered, about 2 hours or until beans are tender.
3 Uncover; cook, stirring occasionally, 30 minutes or until mixture thickens. Serve beans on toasted sourdough bread; sprinkle with parsley.

prep & cook time 2 hours 50 minutes (+ standing)
serves 6
nutritional count per serving 6.3g total fat (1.1g saturated fat); 1626kJ (389 cal); 53.1g carbohydrate; 22.2g protein; 14.5g fibre

Put the kettle on and get the
china teacups — relax and settle
in for a leisurely breakfast.

huevos rancheros

herb omelette with sautéed mushrooms

Huevos rancheros, or 'ranch-style eggs', is a Mexican breakfast traditionally served on farms at a large mid-morning breakfast, or *almuerzo*.

huevos rancheros

3 chorizo sausages (500g), sliced thickly
8 eggs
½ cup (125ml) cream
20g butter
4 x 15cm flour tortillas
1 cup (120g) coarsely grated cheddar cheese
fresh tomato salsa
2 small tomatoes (180g), chopped finely
½ small red onion (50g), chopped finely
1 tablespoon red wine vinegar
1 tablespoon olive oil
¼ cup coarsely chopped fresh coriander

1 Preheat oven to 160°C/140°C fan-forced.
2 Make fresh tomato salsa.
3 Cook chorizo on heated oiled grill plate (or grill or barbecue) until well browned. Drain on absorbent paper; cover to keep warm.
4 Whisk eggs and cream in medium bowl. Melt butter in medium frying pan; cook egg mixture over low heat, stirring gently, until creamy.
5 Meanwhile, place tortillas on oven tray, sprinkle with cheese; warm in oven until cheese melts.
6 Divide tortillas among serving plates; top with egg, chorizo and salsa.
fresh tomato salsa Combine tomatoes, onion, vinegar and oil in small bowl; cover, stand 15 minutes. Stir in coriander just before serving.

prep & cook time 30 minutes (+ standing) **serves** 4
nutritional count per serving 81.7g total fat (35.8g saturated fat); 4126kJ (987 cal); 16.2g carbohydrate; 48.2g protein; 1.9g fibre

herb omelette with sautéed mushrooms

2 tablespoons finely chopped fresh flat-leaf parsley
2 tablespoons finely chopped fresh chervil
2 tablespoons finely chopped fresh chives
2 tablespoons finely chopped fresh tarragon
50g butter
2 tablespoons olive oil
250g swiss brown mushrooms, halved
½ cup (125ml) water
2 teaspoons finely grated lemon rind
1 tablespoon lemon juice
12 eggs

1 Combine herbs in small bowl.
2 Heat 30g of the butter and 1 tablespoon of the oil in large deep frying pan. Add mushrooms; cook, stirring, 5 minutes. Stir in 2 tablespoons of the water; cook, stirring, until water evaporates and mushrooms are tender. Remove pan from heat; stir in rind, juice and 2 tablespoons of the herb mixture. Cover to keep warm.
3 Gently whisk eggs and remaining water in a large bowl; whisk in remaining herb mixture.
4 Heat a quarter of the remaining butter and 1 teaspoon of the remaining oil in medium frying pan. When butter mixture bubbles, pour a quarter of the egg mixture into pan; cook over medium heat, tilting pan, until egg is almost set. Tilt pan backwards; fold omelette in half. Cook 30 seconds then slide onto serving plate.
5 Repeat process with remaining butter, oil and egg mixture, wiping out pan before each addition to make a total of 4 omelettes. Serve omelettes topped with sautéed mushrooms.

prep & cook time 30 minutes **serves** 4
nutritional count per serving 35.3g total fat (12.9g saturated fat); 1714kJ (410 cal); 1g carbohydrate; 22.4g protein; 1.8g fibre

The classic bacon and egg roll gets a sophisticated makeover in this grown-up Italian version.

italian egg, prosciutto and cheese roll

4 eggs
4 focaccia rolls (440g), split
120g taleggio or fontina cheese, sliced thinly
4 slices (60g) prosciutto
8 large fresh basil leaves
tomato sauce
400g can crushed tomatoes
¼ cup (60ml) red wine vinegar
2 tablespoons brown sugar

1 Make tomato sauce.
2 Preheat grill.
3 Fry eggs in heated oiled medium frying pan until cooked as you like.
4 Spread bottom half of each roll with about one tablespoon of the tomato sauce; place on oven tray. Layer cheese and prosciutto on rolls; grill until cheese starts to melt. Top each with 2 basil leaves, an egg and remaining tomato sauce; top with remaining roll half.

tomato sauce Place undrained tomatoes with remaining ingredients in medium saucepan; bring to the boil. Reduce heat; simmer 15 minutes.

prep & cook time 20 minutes **serves** 4
nutritional count per serving 20.3g total fat (9g saturated fat); 2245kJ (537 cal); 58.8g carbohydrate; 27.5g protein; 4.1g fibre

eggs and smoked salmon on blini

8 eggs
200g sliced smoked salmon
2 tablespoons sour cream
1 tablespoon coarsely chopped fresh chives
blini
⅓ cup (50g) buckwheat flour
2 tablespoons plain flour
1 teaspoon baking powder
1 egg
½ cup (125ml) buttermilk
30g butter, melted

1 Make blini.

2 Half-fill a large frying pan with water; bring to the boil. Break 1 egg into cup then slide into pan. Working quickly, repeat process with 3 more eggs. When all 4 eggs are in pan, return water to the boil. Cover pan, turn off heat; stand about 4 minutes or until a light film of white sets over each yolk. Using a slotted spoon, remove eggs one at a time from pan; place spoon on absorbent-paper-lined saucer to blot up poaching liquid. Repeat process to poach remaining 4 eggs.

3 Serve blini topped with eggs, salmon, sour cream and chives.

blini Sift flours and baking powder into medium bowl; gradually whisk in combined egg and buttermilk until mixture is smooth. Stir in butter. Cook blini, in batches, by dropping 1 tablespoon of the batter into heated oiled large frying pan. Cook blini until browned both sides; you will have 12 blini. Cover to keep warm.

prep & cook time 40 minutes **serves** 4
nutritional count per serving 25.9g total fat (11.3g saturated fat); 1731kJ (414 cal); 14.1g carbohydrate; 31.5g protein; 1.6g fibre

creamy scrambled eggs

8 eggs
½ cup (125ml) cream
2 tablespoons finely chopped fresh chives
30g butter

1 Place eggs, cream and chives in medium bowl; beat lightly with fork.
2 Heat butter in large frying pan over medium heat. Add egg mixture, wait a few seconds, then use a wide spatula to gently scrape the set egg mixture along the base of the pan; cook until creamy and barely set. Serve immediately, with toast.

prep & cook time 20 minutes **serves** 4
nutritional count per serving 30.2g total fat (16.2g saturated fat); 1375kJ (329 cal); 1.3g carbohydrate; 14g protein; 0g fibre

cooked english breakfast

50g butter
300g button mushrooms, halved
8 chipolata sausages (240g)
4 rindless bacon rashers (260g)
2 medium tomatoes (300g), halved
1 tablespoon vegetable oil
8 eggs

1 Melt butter in medium saucepan; cook mushrooms, stirring, about 5 minutes or until tender.
2 Cook sausages and bacon in heated oiled large frying pan. Remove from pan; cover to keep warm. Drain fat from pan.
3 Preheat grill. Place tomato, cut-side up, on oven tray; grill tomato until browned lightly.
4 Meanwhile, heat oil in same large frying pan, add eggs; cook eggs until done to your liking.
5 Serve mushrooms, sausages, bacon, tomato and eggs with toast.

prep & cook time 20 minutes **serves** 4
nutritional count per serving 47.7g total fat (20.2g saturated fat); 2424kJ (580 cal); 3.5g carbohydrate; 34.6g protein; 2.4g fibre

serving idea Accompany these baked eggs with some fresh cherry tomatoes and toast.

These may be small but they pack a flavour punch. Don't be tempted to add salt — the prosciutto and fetta are quite salty enough.

prosciutto and fetta baked eggs

12 slices prosciutto (180g)
¼ cup (35g) finely chopped drained semi-dried
   tomatoes in oil
50g fetta cheese, crumbled
2 tablespoons coarsely chopped fresh basil
2 tablespoons coarsely chopped fresh chives
6 eggs

1 Preheat oven to 200°C/180°C fan-forced. Oil six-hole (⅓-cup/80ml) muffin pan.
2 Wrap one prosciutto slice around edge of each pan hole, lay another slice to cover bases; press firmly to seal edges to form a cup.
3 Combine tomato, cheese and herbs in medium bowl; divide half the mixture between prosciutto cups. Break an egg into each cup. Sprinkle with remaining cheese mixture.
4 Bake about 12 minutes or until eggs are cooked. Remove carefully from pan. Serve top-side up.

prep & cook time 30 minutes makes 6
nutritional count per baked egg 9.4g total fat (3.6g saturated fat); 635kJ (152 cal); 2.3g carbohydrate; 14.3g protein; 0.9g fibre

serving idea Serve these
fritters with tomato chutney
and fresh coriander leaves.

For the sweetest and most delicious corn, select cobs with fresh, green husks and bright, plump kernels.

corn fritters

1 cup (150g) self-raising flour
½ teaspoon bicarbonate of soda
1 teaspoon ground cumin
¾ cup (180ml) milk
2 eggs, separated
2 cups (330g) fresh corn kernels
2 green onions, sliced finely
2 tablespoons finely chopped fresh coriander

1 Sift flour, soda and cumin into medium bowl. Gradually whisk in milk and egg yolks until batter is smooth.
2 Beat egg whites in small bowl with electric mixer until soft peaks form.
3 Stir corn, onion and coriander into batter; fold in egg whites.
4 Pour 2 tablespoons of the batter for each fritter into heated oiled large frying pan; spread batter into round shape. Cook fritters about 2 minutes each side. Remove from pan; cover to keep warm. Repeat with remaining batter to make a total of 18 fritters.

prep & cook time 40 minutes **makes** 18
nutritional count per fritter 1.3g total fat (0.5g saturated fat); 263kJ (63 cal); 9.9g carbohydrate; 2.7g protein; 1.2g fibre

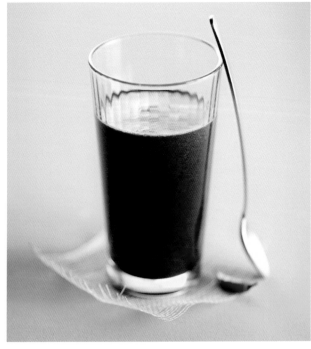

cranberry cooler

1⅓ cups (150g) frozen cranberries, thawed
1kg watermelon, peeled, chopped coarsely
2 lebanese cucumbers (260g), chopped coarsely
2 medium pears (460g), chopped coarsely

1 Push ingredients through juice extractor into glass; stir to combine.

prep time 10 minutes **makes** 1 litre (4 cups)
nutritional count per 250ml 0.2g total fat (0g saturated fat); 134kJ (32 cal); 6.6g carbohydrate; 0.3g protein; 1.2g fibre

zesty beetroot juice

You need 2kg of silver beet to get the required amount of trimmed leaves.

3 medium beetroots (525g), chopped coarsely
4 medium oranges (960g), peeled, quartered
500g trimmed silver beet
1 cup (250ml) water
1 fresh small red thai chilli, chopped finely

1 Push beetroot, orange and silver beet through juice extractor into glass. Stir in the water.
2 Add chilli; stand 5 minutes. Strain mixture through fine sieve into large jug.

prep time 10 minutes **makes** 1 litre (4 cups)
nutritional count per 250ml 0.5g total fat (0g saturated fat); 617kJ (147 cal); 24.5g carbohydrate; 5.8g protein; 10.4g fibre

ruby red citrus juice

2 medium ruby red grapefruits (700g),
   peeled, quartered
3 large oranges (900g), peeled, quartered
1 medium lemon (140g), peeled, quartered
1 cup (250ml) water
2 tablespoons honey

1 Push fruit through juice extractor into glass.
Add the water and honey; stir to combine.

prep time 10 minutes **makes** 1 litre (4 cups)
nutritional count per 250ml 0.4g total fat (0g
saturated fat); 579kJ (138 cal); 28.3g carbohydrate;
2.8g protein; 4.4g fibre

honeydew, papaya and orange juice

1 medium honeydew melon (1.5 kg), peeled,
   chopped coarsely
1 small papaya (650g), peeled, chopped coarsely
3 medium oranges (720g), peeled, quartered

1 Push fruit through juice extractor into glass;
stir to combine.

prep time 10 minutes **makes** 1 litre (4 cups)
nutritional count per 250ml 0.2g total fat (0g
saturated fat); 150kJ (36 cal); 6.9g carbohydrate;
0.7g protein; 1.5g fibre

Hollandaise sauce can be made in advance and reheated gently (and very carefully) over simmering water, stirring constantly.

eggs benedict

8 eggs
4 english muffins
200g shaved leg ham
¼ cup finely chopped fresh chives
hollandaise sauce
1½ tablespoons white wine vinegar
1 tablespoon lemon juice
½ teaspoon black peppercorns
2 egg yolks
125g unsalted butter, melted

1 Make hollandaise sauce.
2 To poach eggs, half-fill a large shallow frying pan with water; bring to the boil. Break 1 egg into a cup, then slide into pan; repeat with three more eggs. When all eggs are in pan, allow water to return to the boil. Cover pan, turn off heat; stand about 4 minutes or until a light film of egg white sets over yolks. Remove the egg with a slotted spoon and drain on absorbent paper; cover to keep warm. Repeat with remaining eggs.
3 Meanwhile, split muffins in half and toast.
4 Serve muffins topped with ham, poached eggs, sauce and chives.

hollandaise sauce Combine vinegar, juice and peppercorns in small saucepan; bring to the boil. Reduce heat; simmer, uncovered, until liquid is reduced by half. Strain through a fine sieve into small heatproof bowl; cool 10 minutes. Whisk egg yolks into vinegar mixture. Set bowl over small saucepan of simmering water; do not allow water to touch base of bowl. Whisk mixture over heat until thickened. Remove bowl from heat; gradually whisk in melted butter in a thin steady stream, whisking constantly until sauce is thick and creamy.

prep & cook time 50 minutes **serves** 4
nutritional count per serving 40.6g total fat (21.2g saturated fat); 2450kJ (586 cal); 24.2g carbohydrate; 30.8g protein; 2g fibre

berry yogurt muffins

banana bread

berry yogurt muffins

We used a mixture of raspberries and blueberries in these muffins.

1½ cups (225g) self-raising flour
⅓ cup (30g) rolled oats
3 eggs
¾ cup (165g) firmly packed brown sugar
¾ cup (200g) yogurt
⅓ cup (80ml) vegetable oil
180g fresh or frozen berries

1 Preheat oven to 200°C/180°C fan-forced. Grease six-hole (¾-cup/180ml) texas muffin pan.
2 Combine sifted flour with oats in medium bowl. Stir in eggs, sugar, yogurt and oil; add berries, stir gently into muffin mixture.
3 Spoon mixture into pan holes; bake about 20 minutes. Stand 5 minutes before turning, top-side up, onto wire rack to cool.

prep & cook time 30 minutes **serves** 6
nutritional count per muffin 16.9g total fat (3.2g saturated fat); 1806kJ (432 cal); 58.8g carbohydrate; 9.7g protein; 2.5g fibre

banana bread

You need two large overripe bananas (460g) for this recipe.

90g unsalted butter, softened
1 teaspoon vanilla extract
1 cup (220g) firmly packed brown sugar
2 eggs
1 cup mashed banana
1 cup (150g) plain flour
1 cup (150g) self-raising flour

1 Preheat oven to 180°C/160°C fan-forced. Grease 14cm x 21cm loaf pan; line base and long sides with baking paper, extending paper 5cm above long sides.
2 Beat butter, extract and sugar in small bowl with electric mixer until light and fluffy. Beat in eggs, one at a time. Transfer mixture to large bowl; stir in banana then sifted flours, in two batches.
3 Spread mixture into pan; cover with a strip of pleated foil. Bake 40 minutes; uncover, bake about 30 minutes. Stand 5 minutes; lift onto wire rack to cool. Serve toasted or warm, with butter.

prep & cook time 1 hour 20 minutes **makes** 12 slices
nutritional count per slice 9.5g total fat (5.6g saturated fat); 1296kJ (309 cal); 49.7g carbohydrate; 5.1g protein; 1.7g fibre

blueberry buttermilk hotcakes with bacon

2 cups (300g) self-raising flour
¼ cup (55g) caster sugar
2 eggs
600ml buttermilk
50g butter, melted
1 cup (150g) fresh blueberries
cooking-oil spray
12 thin rindless bacon rashers (360g)
½ cup (125ml) maple syrup

1 Sift flour and sugar into large bowl. Whisk eggs, buttermilk and butter in large jug. Gradually whisk egg mixture into flour mixture until smooth. Stir in berries, pour batter into large jug.
2 Spray large heavy-based frying pan with cooking oil. Pour ¼-cup batter for each pancake into heated pan (you can cook four at a time). Cook pancakes until bubbles appear on the surface; turn, brown other side. Cover to keep warm.
3 Repeat process using cooking oil and remaining batter, wiping out pan between batches, to make 14 more pancakes.
4 Meanwhile, heat oiled large frying pan; cook bacon until crisp.
5 Drizzle pancakes with syrup, serve with bacon.

prep & cook time 35 minutes **serves** 6
nutritional count per serving 15.4g total fat (7.7g saturated fat); 2224kJ (532 cal); 71.8g carbohydrate; 24.5g protein; 2.4g fibre

Make sure you use real maple syrup here. It is very different from 'maple-flavoured' syrup, and well worth the extra cost.

french toast

bircher muesli

french toast

4 eggs
½ cup (125ml) cream
¼ cup (60ml) milk
1 teaspoon ground cinnamon
¼ cup (55g) caster sugar
100g butter, melted
8 thick slices white bread (360g)
2 tablespoons icing sugar
⅓ cup (80ml) maple syrup

1 Whisk eggs in medium bowl, then whisk in cream, milk, cinnamon and sugar.
2 Heat a quarter of the butter in medium frying pan. Dip two bread slices into egg mixture, one at a time; cook bread until browned both sides. Remove french toast from pan; keep warm.
3 Repeat step 2 to make a total of 8 french toasts.
4 Serve toasts dusted with sifted icing sugar and drizzled with maple syrup. Serve, topped with sliced strawberries.

prep & cook time 20 minutes **serves** 4
nutritional count per serving 42.2g total fat (24.8g saturated fat); 3194kJ (764 cal); 79.4g carbohydrate; 15.5g protein; 2.6g fibre

bircher muesli

2 cups (180g) rolled oats
1¼ cups (310ml) apple juice
1 cup (280g) yogurt
2 medium green-skinned apples (300g)
¼ cup (35g) roasted slivered almonds
¼ cup (40g) dried currants
¼ cup (20g) toasted shredded coconut
1 teaspoon ground cinnamon
½ cup (140g) yogurt, extra

1 Combine oats, juice and yogurt in medium bowl. Cover; refrigerate overnight.
2 Peel, core and coarsely grate one apple; stir into oat mixture with nuts, currants, coconut and cinnamon.
3 Core and thinly slice remaining apple. Serve muesli topped with extra yogurt and apple slices.

prep time 10 minutes (+ refrigeration) **serves** 6
nutritional count per serving 9.2g total fat (3g saturated fat); 1120kJ (268 cal); 36.1g carbohydrate; 8.1g protein; 3.9g fibre

Dr Bircher-Benner, a physician and pioneer in nutritional research, introduced his now famous muesli to the patients at his clinic in Zurich, Switzerland in the early 20th Century.

serving idea These muffins are delicious eaten still warm with a good slab of butter. Serve them alongside a fresh fruit platter and a pot of piping hot coffee or tea.

The beauty of these muffins is that you prepare the mixture the night before, then all you have to do in the morning is pop them in the oven.

overnight bran muffins

1 egg
1¼ cups (185g) plain flour
1 teaspoon ground cinnamon
1 teaspoon bicarbonate of soda
½ cup (110g) firmly packed brown sugar
1¾ cups (105g) unprocessed bran
¾ cup (105g) coarsely chopped seedless
   fresh or dried dates
1½ cups (375ml) buttermilk
½ cup (125ml) vegetable oil

1 Whisk egg in medium bowl, stir in remaining ingredients. (Do not over-mix; mixture should be lumpy.) Cover mixture, refrigerate overnight.
2 Preheat oven to 200°C/180°C fan-forced. Grease 12-hole (⅓-cup/80ml) muffin pan.
3 Spoon muffin mixture into pan holes; bake about 20 minutes. Stand muffins in pan 5 minutes before turning, top-side up, onto wire rack to cool. Serve with butter.

prep & cook time 30 minutes (+ refrigeration)
makes 12
nutritional count per muffin 11.3g total fat (1.9g saturated fat); 1037kJ (248 cal); 28.7g carbohydrate; 5.2g protein; 5.3g fibre

midweek meals

These meals are perfect after a long day, when time is of the essence.

Don't be afraid of poaching fish
— it's quick, easy, and produces
a wonderfully tender, moist result.

poached trout and potato salad

800g kipfler potatoes, unpeeled, halved

1 litre (4 cups) water

4 x 5cm strips lemon rind

2 sprigs fresh dill

600g ocean trout fillets

1 small red onion (100g), sliced thinly

1 lebanese cucumber (130g),
  seeded, sliced thinly

50g rocket leaves

lemon and dill dressing

⅓ cup (80ml) olive oil

¼ cup (60ml) lemon juice

1 clove garlic, crushed

1 tablespoon finely chopped fresh dill

1 tablespoon drained, rinsed baby capers

1 Boil, steam or microwave potato until tender; drain.

2 Place the water, rind and dill in medium saucepan; bring to the boil. Add fish; simmer, covered, about 10 minutes or until cooked as desired. Drain fish; discard cooking liquid. Flake fish coarsely into large bowl; discard skin.

3 Meanwhile, make lemon and dill dressing.

4 Add potato, dressing and remaining ingredients to bowl of fish; toss gently to combine.

lemon and dill dressing Place ingredients in screw-top jar; shake well.

prep & cook time 25 minutes **serves** 4

nutritional count per serving 24.3g total fat (3.9g saturated fat); 2031kJ (486 cal); 29.3g carbohydrate; 34.9g protein; 5.1g fibre

garlic seafood stir-fry

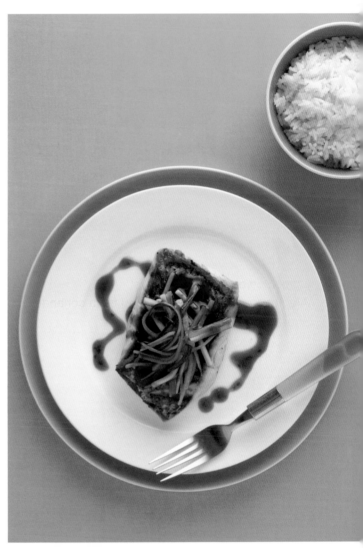

snapper fillets with ginger soy syrup

garlic seafood stir-fry

1kg uncooked medium king prawns
500g cleaned baby squid hoods
¼ cup (60ml) peanut oil
1 tablespoon finely chopped coriander
   root and stem mixture
2 fresh small red thai chillies
½ teaspoon coarsely ground black pepper
4 cloves garlic, crushed
170g asparagus, trimmed, chopped coarsely
175g broccolini, chopped coarsely
1 cup (80g) bean sprouts
2 green onions, sliced thinly
2 tablespoons coarsely chopped fresh coriander
1 lime, cut into wedges

1 Shell and devein prawns, leaving tails intact.
2 Cut squid down centre to open out; score inside in diagonal pattern then cut into thick strips.
3 Heat half the oil in wok; cook seafood, in batches, until prawns change in colour.
4 Heat remaining oil in wok; stir-fry coriander mixture, chilli, pepper and garlic until fragrant. Add asparagus and broccolini; cook, stirring, until vegetables are almost tender. Return seafood to wok with sprouts; stir-fry until hot.
5 Serve stir-fry sprinkled with green onion and coriander, accompanied with lime.

prep & cook time 40 minutes **serves** 4
nutritional count per serving 16.2g total fat (3.1g saturated fat); 1509kJ (361 cal); 1.6g carbohydrate; 50.3g protein; 3.7g fibre

snapper fillets with ginger soy syrup

2 medium carrots (240g), cut into matchsticks
2 medium zucchini (240g), cut into matchsticks
4 x 275g snapper fillets, skin on
1 cup (250ml) bottled sweet chilli, ginger and
   soy marinade

1 Boil, steam or microwave carrot and zucchini, separately, until tender.
2 Meanwhile, score fish skin. Cook fish, skin-side down, in heated oiled large frying pan about 5 minutes. Turn fish; cook about 3 minutes. Remove from pan.
3 Add ⅓ cup (80ml) water and marinade to same pan; stir until hot.
4 Serve fish with sauce and vegetables. Serve with steamed jasmine rice.

prep & cook time 20 minutes **serves** 4
nutritional count per serving 4.6g total fat (1.7g saturated fat); 1304kJ (312 cal); 5.4g carbohydrate; 60.4g protein; 2.4g fibre

cranberry and pine nut pilaf with chicken

30g butter
1 tablespoon olive oil
1 medium brown onion (150g), chopped finely
1 stalk celery (150g), trimmed, chopped finely
1½ cups (300g) basmati rice, rinsed, drained
1 bay leaf
1 cinnamon stick
1 litre (4 cups) chicken stock
⅔ cup (160ml) water
400g chicken breast fillets
1 cup (250ml) dry white wine
⅓ cup (45g) dried cranberries
30g butter, extra
⅓ cup (50g) roasted pine nuts
1 tablespoon lemon juice

1 Melt butter with half the oil in medium saucepan; cook onion and celery, stirring, until celery softens. Add rice, bay leaf and cinnamon stick; cook, stirring, 2 minutes. Add stock and the water; bring to the boil. Reduce heat; simmer, covered, about 15 minutes or until rice is tender and liquid is absorbed.
2 Meanwhile, heat remaining oil in a large frying pan. Cook chicken until browned and cooked through. Remove from heat. Cover to keep warm.
3 Pour wine into same pan; bring to the boil. Reduce heat; simmer, uncovered, until liquid is reduced by half. Stir in cranberries and extra butter; add to rice mixture, stir until combined.
4 Fluff pilaf with fork; stir in nuts and juice. Serve with sliced chicken.

prep & cook time 40 minutes **serves** 4
nutritional count per serving 29.5g total fat (10.5g saturated fat); 3068kJ (734 cal); 72.2g carbohydrate; 33.2g protein; 2.7g fibre

serving idea Steamed beans are delicious with a drizzle of extra virgin olive oil, a squeeze of lemon and a sprinkle of sea salt.

This bistro-style meal is robust, simple and perfect for casual dining.

peppered fillet steaks with creamy bourbon sauce

4 x 125g beef fillet steaks
2 teaspoons cracked black pepper
2 tablespoons olive oil
6 shallots (150g), sliced thinly
1 clove garlic, crushed
⅓ cup (80ml) bourbon
¼ cup (60ml) beef stock
2 teaspoons dijon mustard
300ml cream

1 Rub beef all over with pepper. Heat half the oil in large frying pan; cook beef, uncovered, until cooked as desired. Remove from pan; cover to keep warm.
2 Heat remaining oil in same pan; cook shallot and garlic, stirring, until shallot softens. Add bourbon; stir until mixture simmers and starts to thicken. Add remaining ingredients; bring to the boil. Reduce heat; simmer, uncovered, about 5 minutes or until sauce thickens slightly.
3 Place beef on serving plates, drizzle with sauce; serve with fried potatoes and steamed green beans.

prep & cook time 20 minutes **serves** 4
nutritional count per serving 49.3g total fat (25.9g saturated fat); 2742kJ (656 cal); 13.2g carbohydrate; 28.7g protein; 0.7g fibre

chilli-garlic mince with snake beans

2 cloves garlic, quartered

2 long green chillies, chopped coarsely

2 fresh small red thai chillies, chopped coarsely

1 tablespoon peanut oil

600g beef mince

150g snake beans, chopped coarsely

1 medium red capsicum (200g), sliced thinly

2 tablespoons kecap asin

¼ cup (60ml) hoisin sauce

4 green onions, sliced thickly

2 tablespoons crushed peanuts

1 Blend or process garlic and chillies until mixture is finely chopped.

2 Heat half the oil in wok; stir-fry garlic mixture until fragrant. Add beef; stir-fry, in batches, until cooked through.

3 Heat remaining oil in cleaned wok; stir-fry beans and capsicum until tender.

4 Return beef to wok with sauces and onion; stir-fry until hot. Sprinkle over nuts; serve with lime wedges.

prep & cook time 25 minutes **serves** 4
nutritional count per serving 18.6g total fat (5.6g saturated fat); 1476kJ (353 cal); 9.6g carbohydrate; 34.8g protein; 4.2g fibre

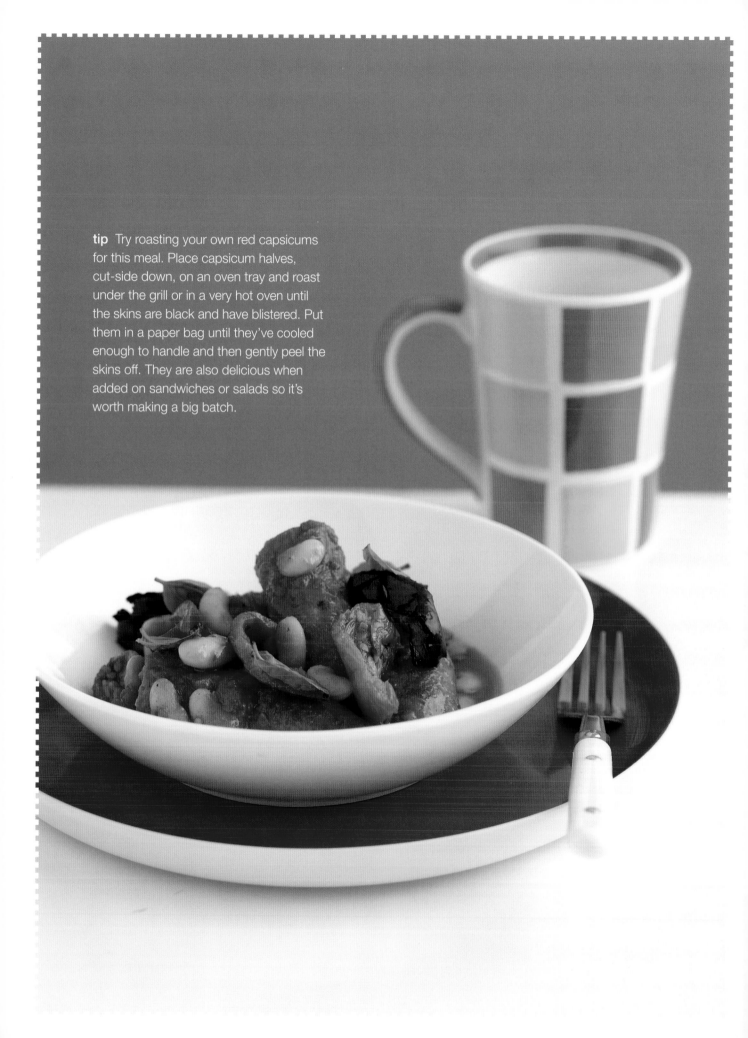

tip Try roasting your own red capsicums for this meal. Place capsicum halves, cut-side down, on an oven tray and roast under the grill or in a very hot oven until the skins are black and have blistered. Put them in a paper bag until they've cooled enough to handle and then gently peel the skins off. They are also delicious when added on sandwiches or salads so it's worth making a big batch.

italian braised sausages with white beans

We used semi-dried tomatoes, marinated artichokes, grilled eggplant and red capsicum for the antipasto mix; however, any combination of vegetables can be used.

8 thick beef sausages (1.2kg)
2 x 400g can diced tomatoes
200g drained marinated antipasto vegetables
400g can cannellini beans, rinsed, drained
½ cup loosely packed fresh baby basil leaves

1 Cook sausages in heated oiled large saucepan until browned. Remove from pan; cut in half lengthways.
2 Add undrained tomatoes and ⅓ cup (80ml) water to same pan; bring to the boil. Return sausages to pan with antipasto vegetables; simmer, covered, 15 minutes.
3 Add beans to pan; simmer, uncovered, about 10 minutes or until thickened slightly.
4 Remove from heat, stir in half the basil; serve topped with remaining basil.

prep & cook time 25 minutes **serves** 4
nutritional count per serving 78.1g total fat (36.9g saturated fat); 4113kJ (983 cal); 23g carbohydrate; 41.9g protein; 16g fibre

spicy veal pizzaiola

lamb cutlets niçoise

herb-crumbed lamb racks

1 cup (70g) stale breadcrumbs
1 tablespoon finely chopped fresh flat-leaf parsley
2 tablespoons finely chopped fresh mint
2 teaspoons finely grated lemon rind
40g butter
2 shallots (50g), chopped finely
4 x 4 french-trimmed lamb cutlet racks (720g)
250g baby vine-ripened truss tomatoes
cooking-oil spray

1 Preheat oven to 220°C/200°C fan-forced.
2 Combine breadcrumbs, herbs and rind in small bowl.
3 Melt butter in small frying pan; pour half the butter into breadcrumb mixture.
4 Cook shallot in remaining butter, stirring, until soft; stir into breadcrumb mixture.
5 Place lamb and tomatoes in oiled large baking dish; spray tomatoes with oil. Press breadcrumb mixture onto lamb. Roast, uncovered, about 15 minutes or until cooked as desired. Serve lamb with roasted tomatoes.

prep & cook time 40 minutes **serves** 4
nutritional count per serving 25g total fat (12.6g saturated fat); 1538kJ (368 cal); 13.7g carbohydrate; 21.4g protein; 1.9g fibre

pork cutlets with caramelised pear sauce

1 tablespoon olive oil
20g butter
6 x 180g french-trimmed pork cutlets
2 tablespoons brown sugar
3 medium pears (700g), cut crossways into 1.5cm-thick slices
¾ cup (180ml) dry white wine
1 cup (250ml) chicken stock
¼ cup coarsely chopped fresh sage

1 Heat oil and half the butter in large heavy-based frying pan; cook pork, in batches, until browned and cooked as desired. Cover to keep warm.
2 Stir sugar and remaining butter into pan; add pear. Cook about 5 minutes; remove from pan.
3 Add wine to pan; simmer, stirring, 2 minutes. Add stock to pan; simmer, uncovered, 10 minutes or until liquid has reduced by half. Return pear to pan with sage; simmer until heated through.
4 Serve pork with pear sauce.

prep & cook time 35 minutes **serves** 6
nutritional count per serving 18.6g total fat (6.6g saturated fat); 1488kJ (356 cal); 18.8g carbohydrate; 22.3g protein; 2.6g fibre

char siu pork with spicy fried noodles

600g pork fillets
½ cup (125ml) char siu sauce
450g fresh wide rice noodles
2 tablespoons peanut oil
350g broccolini, chopped coarsely
2 fresh long red chillies, sliced thinly

1 Combine pork and ⅓ cup of the sauce in medium bowl; refrigerate 10 minutes.
2 Cook pork on heated oiled grill plate (or grill or barbecue) until cooked through.
3 Meanwhile, place noodles in large heatproof bowl, cover with boiling water; separate with fork, drain.
4 Heat oil in wok; stir-fry broccolini and chilli until tender. Add noodles, remaining sauce and about a tablespoon of water to wok; stir-fry until hot.
5 Slice pork; serve with noodle mixture.

prep & cook time 25 minutes **serves** 4
nutritional count per serving 15.1g total fat (3.1g saturated fat); 1927kJ (461 cal); 37.2g carbohydrate; 38.8g protein; 7.7g fibre

Pork fillet is an incredibly lean cut of meat, making this simple, delicious meal healthy as well as easy.

The combination of pork and veal mince gives these meatballs a deliciously rich quality that you won't get with beef mince.

serving idea This hearty Italian-American classic needs nothing more than a simple green salad to follow.

when friends drop by

it's worth having these very impressive recipes at your fingertips.

turkish beetroot dip

3 medium beetroot (500g), trimmed
1 teaspoon caraway seeds
1 teaspoon ground cumin
¼ teaspoon hot paprika
¾ cup (200g) yogurt
½ cup loosely packed fresh mint leaves
2 cloves garlic, crushed
1 tablespoon lemon juice

1 Cook beetroot in medium saucepan of boiling water, uncovered, about 45 minutes or until tender; drain. When cool enough to handle, peel beetroot then chop coarsely.
2 Meanwhile, dry-fry spices in a small frying pan until fragrant; cool.
3 Blend or process beetroot with spices and remaining ingredients until smooth.

prep & cook time 50 minutes **makes** 2 cups
nutritional count per tablespoon 0.3g total fat (0.2g saturated fat); 67kJ (16 cal); 2g carbohydrate; 0.8g protein; 0.7g fibre

warm orange and fennel olives

1 large orange (300g)
400g mixed marinated seeded olives
½ cup (125ml) dry red wine
1 teaspoon coarsely ground black pepper
½ teaspoon fennel seeds

1 Peel thin strips of rind from orange. Combine rind with remaining ingredients in medium saucepan; bring to a simmer. Stand 10 minutes before serving warm.

prep & cook time 10 minutes **serves** 6
nutritional count per serving 2.1g total fat (0.3g saturated fat); 360kJ (86 cal); 12g carbohydrate; 0.6g protein; 1.8g fibre

Put some music on, pour everyone a glass of wine and pull out the nibbles for some casual entertaining.

steamed mussels in tomato garlic broth

1 tablespoon olive oil
2 shallots (50g), chopped finely
4 cloves garlic, crushed
410g can crushed tomatoes
1 cup (250ml) dry white wine
1 teaspoon caster sugar
2kg small black mussels
½ cup coarsely chopped fresh flat-leaf parsley

1 Heat oil in large saucepan; cook shallot and garlic, stirring, until shallot softens.
2 Add undrained tomatoes, wine and sugar; bring to the boil. Reduce heat; simmer, uncovered, about 10 minutes or until sauce thickens slightly.
3 Meanwhile, scrub mussels; remove beards. Add mussels to pan; simmer, covered, about 5 minutes, shaking pan occasionally, until mussels open (discard any that do not). Remove mussels from pan, divide among serving bowls; cover with foil to keep warm.
4 Bring tomato mixture to the boil; boil, uncovered, about 5 minutes or until sauce thickens slightly. Pour tomato mixture over mussels; sprinkle with parsley.

prep & cook time 55 minutes **serves** 4
nutritional count per serving 6.7g total fat (1.2g saturated fat); 828kJ (198 cal); 9.9g carbohydrate; 13.3g protein; 2.2g fibre

italian sausage and three-cheese lasagne

500g italian sausages
250g frozen chopped spinach, thawed, drained
250g ricotta cheese
¼ teaspoon ground nutmeg
½ cup (40g) finely grated parmesan cheese
1 egg
6 sheets fresh lasagne
250g mozzarella cheese, sliced thinly
tomato sauce
1 tablespoon olive oil
1 medium onion (150g), chopped finely
1 medium carrot (120g), chopped finely
1 stalk celery (150g), trimmed, chopped finely
5 x 8cm long parsley stalks, crushed
2 cloves garlic, crushed
½ cup (125ml) dry red wine
¼ cup (70g) tomato paste
700g bottled tomato pasta sauce
cheese sauce
50g butter
⅓ cup (50g) plain flour
2 cups (500ml) milk
1½ cups (120g) finely grated parmesan cheese

1 Make tomato sauce. Make cheese sauce.
2 Preheat oven to 200°C/180°C fan-forced.
3 Cook sausages in oiled large frying pan until browned all over; drain then slice thinly.
4 Combine spinach, ricotta, nutmeg, parmesan and egg in medium bowl.

5 Spread ½ cup of the cheese sauce over base of 20cm x 30cm ovenproof dish. Top with two pasta sheets then spread with half the spinach mixture. Sprinkle with half the sausage; cover with 1 cup of the tomato sauce then half the remaining cheese sauce.
6 Top with two pasta sheets. Spread remaining spinach mixture over pasta; sprinkle with remaining sausage. Spread with 1 cup tomato sauce, then remaining cheese sauce.
7 Top with remaining pasta, then half the remaining tomato sauce. Top with mozzarella; spread with remaining tomato sauce.
8 Bake lasagne, covered, 30 minutes. Uncover, bake about 10 minutes or until browned lightly. Stand 10 minutes before serving.

tomato sauce Heat oil in large saucepan, add onion, carrot, celery and parsley; cook, stirring occasionally, until vegetables soften. Add garlic; cook, stirring, 1 minute. Add wine; cook, stirring, until almost evaporated. Discard parsley stalks. Add paste; cook, stirring, 3 minutes. Add sauce; simmer, uncovered, about 15 minutes.

cheese sauce Melt butter in medium saucepan, add flour; cook, stirring, until mixture thickens and bubbles. Gradually add milk; stir until mixture boils and thickens. Reduce heat; cook, stirring, 1 minute, remove from heat. Add cheese, stir until melted.

prep & cook time 2 hours 40 minutes **serves** 8
nutritional count per serving 46.8g total fat (23.1g saturated fat); 3227kJ (772 cal); 44g carbohydrate; 39.3g protein; 5.4g fibre

strawberries in rosewater syrup

sticky banana puddings with butterscotch sauce

affogato with frangelico

⅓ cup (30g) ground espresso coffee beans
1½ cups (375ml) boiling water
12 small scoops of vanilla ice-cream
½ cup (125ml) Frangelico

1 Place coffee in coffee plunger; add boiling water, stand 4 minutes before plunging.

2 Place 2 small scoops of ice-cream in each of 6 small heatproof glasses or coffee cups; pour 1 tablespoon of the Frangelico over each.

3 Give the hot coffee to the guests to pour over the ice-cream.

prep time 10 minutes **serves** 6
nutritional count per serving 6.4g total fat (4.2g saturated fat); 723kJ (173 cal); 20.2g carbohydrate; 2.1g protein; 0g fibre

black-eyed bean and ham soup

1 cup (200g) black-eyed beans
1 tablespoon olive oil
1 stalk celery (150g), trimmed, chopped coarsely
1 small brown onion (80g), chopped coarsely
1 medium carrot (120g), chopped coarsely
1 bay leaf
2 cloves garlic
1.2kg ham hock
1 litre (4 cups) chicken stock
2 litres (8 cups) water
½ bunch trimmed silver beet (125g), shredded finely
2 tablespoons cider vinegar

1 Place beans in medium bowl, cover with water; stand overnight, rinse, drain.
2 Heat oil in large saucepan, add celery, onion and carrot; cook until vegetables are soft. Add bay leaf, garlic, ham hock, stock and the water; bring to the boil. Reduce heat; simmer, uncovered, 1 hour.
3 Add beans to soup; simmer, uncovered, 1 hour or until beans are tender.
4 Remove hock from soup. When cool enough to handle, remove meat from hock. Discard bone; shred meat coarsely, return to soup.
5 Add silver beet to soup; cook, stirring, until wilted. Remove from heat; stir in vinegar.

prep & cook time 2 hours 50 minutes (+ standing)
serves 6
nutritional count per serving 7.2g total fat (1.8g saturated fat); 945kJ (226 cal); 16.1g carbohydrate; 21.2g protein; 6.3g fibre

french onion soup with gruyère croûtons

50g butter
4 large brown onions (800g), sliced thinly
¾ cup (180ml) dry white wine
3 cups (750ml) water
1 litre (4 cups) beef stock
1 bay leaf
1 tablespoon plain flour
1 teaspoon fresh thyme leaves
gruyère croûtons
1 small french bread (150g), cut in 1.5cm slices
½ cup (60g) coarsely grated gruyère cheese

1 Melt butter in large saucepan, add onion; cook, stirring occasionally, about 30 minutes or until caramelised.
2 Meanwhile, bring wine to the boil in large saucepan; boil 1 minute then stir in the water, stock and bay leaf; return to the boil. Remove from heat.
3 Stir flour into onion mixture; cook, stirring, 2 minutes. Gradually add hot broth mixture to onion mixture, stirring, until mixture boils and thickens slightly. Reduce heat; simmer, uncovered, stirring occasionally, 20 minutes. Discard bay leaf; stir in thyme.
4 Meanwhile, make gruyère croûtons.
5 Serve bowls of soup topped with croûtons. Sprinkle with extra thyme leaves, if you like.
gruyère croûtons Preheat grill. Toast bread on one side then turn and sprinkle with cheese; grill croûtons until cheese browns lightly.

prep & cook time 1 hour 10 minutes serves 4
nutritional count per serving 16.7g total fat (10g saturated fat); 1522kJ (364 cal); 31.1g carbohydrate; 13.4g protein; 3.9g fibre

chicken, pea and asparagus soup with pistou

*You need 450g of fresh peas in the pod or
2 cups (240g) frozen peas for this recipe.*

3 cups (750ml) chicken stock
3 cups (750ml) water
1 clove garlic, crushed
¼ teaspoon coarsely ground black pepper
400g chicken breast fillets
170g asparagus, trimmed, chopped coarsely
1½ cups (240g) shelled fresh peas
1 tablespoon lemon juice
pistou
½ cup coarsely chopped fresh flat-leaf parsley
½ cup coarsely chopped fresh mint
¼ cup coarsely chopped fresh garlic chives
2 teaspoons finely grated lemon rind
1 clove garlic, crushed
2 teaspoons olive oil

1 Bring stock, the water, garlic and pepper to the boil in large saucepan. Add chicken; return to boil. Reduce heat; simmer, covered, about 10 minutes or until chicken is cooked through. Cool in poaching liquid 10 minutes. Remove chicken from pan; slice thinly.
2 Meanwhile, make pistou.
3 Add remaining ingredients to soup; bring to the boil. Return chicken to pan; simmer, uncovered, about 3 minutes or until vegetables are just tender.
4 Divide soup among serving bowls; top with pistou.
pistou Using mortar and pestle, pound ingredients until smooth.

prep & cook time 30 minutes **serves** 4
nutritional count per serving 5.7g total fat (1.3g saturated fat); 861kJ (206 cal); 7.3g carbohydrate; 28.9g protein; 4.4g fibre

Pistou is France's much-loved answer to pesto, and like most classic French dishes with several versions, there is much squabbling between various towns and regions about whose version is best.

note Pistou is most commonly associated with a Provençal summer vegetable soup, but is also delicious served on pasta dishes or spread on thick slices of crusty bread.

chicken and leek pie

veal goulash and potato pies

roast chicken with tomato-braised beans

roast chicken with herb stuffing

Roast chicken is one of those foods that everyone loves but few actually make themselves. Try either of these recipes and you'll see how easy and satisfying it is to make.

roast chicken with tomato-braised beans

2kg chicken
1 medium lemon (140g), quartered
6 sprigs fresh thyme
6 cloves garlic, unpeeled
60g butter, softened
2 tablespoons lemon juice
2 cloves garlic, crushed
2 teaspoons finely chopped fresh thyme
1 cup (250ml) water
1 tablespoon olive oil
1 medium brown onion (150g), chopped coarsely
1kg green beans, trimmed
4 medium tomatoes (600g), chopped coarsely

1 Preheat oven to 200°C/180°C fan-forced.
2 Tuck wing tips under chicken. Fill cavity with lemon, thyme sprigs and garlic, fold skin over to enclose filling; secure with toothpicks. Tie legs together with kitchen string.
3 Combine butter, juice, crushed garlic and chopped thyme in small bowl; rub mixture all over chicken.
4 Place chicken on oiled rack in large baking dish; pour the water into dish. Roast about 2 hours, basting occasionally with pan juices.
5 Meanwhile, heat oil in large saucepan; cook onion, stirring, until onion softens. Add beans and tomato; cook, covered, stirring occasionally, about 20 minutes or until vegetables soften slightly.
6 Serve chicken with beans.

prep & cook time 2 hours 40 minutes **serves** 6
nutritional count per serving 33.5g total fat (12.7g saturated fat); 2123kJ (508 cal); 8.3g carbohydrate; 40.3g protein; 7.3g fibre

roast chicken with herb stuffing

1.5kg chicken
20g butter, melted
herb stuffing
1½ cups (105g) stale breadcrumbs
1 stalk celery (150g), trimmed, chopped finely
1 small white onion (100g), chopped finely
1 teaspoon dried mixed herbs
1 egg, beaten lightly
50g butter, melted

1 Preheat oven to 200°C/180°C fan-forced.
2 Make herb stuffing. Fill chicken cavity with stuffing, fold over skin to enclose; secure with toothpicks. Tie legs together with kitchen string.
3 Place chicken on rack over baking dish half-filled with water (water should not touch chicken). Brush chicken with melted butter; roast 15 minutes. Reduce oven to 180°C/160°C fan-forced; roast chicken about 1½ hours or until cooked through.
4 Stand chicken 10 minutes before serving. Serve chicken with steamed asparagus and roasted baby new potatoes.
herb stuffing Combine ingredients in medium bowl.

prep & cook time 2 hours 15 minutes **serves** 4
nutritional count per serving 46.8g total fat (19.4g saturated fat); 2817kJ (674 cal); 19.7g carbohydrate; 43.4g protein; 1.9g fibre

roast beef with yorkshire puddings

2kg corner piece beef topside roast
2 cups (500ml) dry red wine
2 bay leaves
6 black peppercorns
¼ cup (70g) wholegrain mustard
4 cloves garlic, sliced
4 sprigs fresh thyme
1 medium brown onion (150g), chopped coarsely
2 medium carrots (240g), chopped coarsely
1 large leek (500g), chopped coarsely
2 stalks celery (300g), trimmed, chopped coarsely
2 tablespoons olive oil

yorkshire puddings
1 cup (150g) plain flour
2 eggs
½ cup (125ml) milk
½ cup (125ml) water

gravy
2 tablespoons plain flour
1½ cups (375ml) beef stock

1 Combine beef, wine, bay leaves, peppercorns, mustard, garlic, thyme and onion in large bowl; cover, refrigerate 3 hours or overnight.
2 Preheat oven to 180°C/160°C fan-forced.
3 Drain beef over medium bowl; reserve 1 cup (250ml) of marinade. Combine carrot, leek and celery in large baking dish, top with beef; brush beef with oil.
4 Roast beef, uncovered, about 1½ hours. Remove beef from dish, wrap in foil; stand beef 20 minutes before serving.
5 Increase oven to 220°C/200°C fan-forced.
6 Remove vegetables with slotted spoon; discard vegetables. Pour pan juices into jug; stand 2 minutes. Reserve 1½ tablespoons oil for yorkshire puddings, pour off excess oil; reserve 2 tablespoons of pan juices for gravy.
7 Make yorkshire puddings and gravy.
8 Serve beef with yorkshire puddings and gravy; accompany with roasted potatoes and steamed baby carrots.

yorkshire puddings Sift flour into medium bowl; whisk in combined eggs, milk and water all at once until smooth. Stand batter 30 minutes. Divide reserved oil between eight holes of 12-hole (⅓-cup/80ml) muffin pan; heat in oven 2 minutes. Divide batter among pan holes. Bake about 20 minutes or until puddings are puffed and golden.

gravy Heat reserved pan juices in same baking dish, add flour; cook, stirring, until browned. Gradually add stock and reserved marinade; cook, stirring, until mixture boils and thickens. Strain gravy into heatproof jug.

prep & cook time 2 hours 35 minutes (+ refrigeration & standing) **serves** 8
nutritional count per serving 15.4g total fat (4.8g saturated fat); 2169kJ (519 cal); 21.1g carbohydrate; 61.2g protein; 4g fibre

pot-roasted pork with apple and sage

1 tablespoon olive oil
1.5kg piece pork neck
600g spring onions, stems trimmed
   to 10cm lengths
6 large sprigs fresh sage
6 large sprigs fresh thyme
1 cup (250ml) dry white wine
2 tablespoons boiling water
40g butter
3 large apples (600g), unpeeled, cored,
   cut into thick wedges

1 Cook pork with 2 teaspoons of the oil in large heavy-based saucepan, turning, until browned all over. Add onions, herbs and wine to pan; bring to the boil. Reduce heat; simmer, covered tightly, about 1½ hours or until pork is cooked, turning pork twice during cooking time. Transfer pork and onions to serving platter; cover to keep warm.
2 Strain pan juices into serving jug; discard solids. Stir the water into jug; cover to keep sauce warm.
3 Meanwhile, heat butter and remaining oil in large frying pan; cook apple, stirring, about 10 minutes or until tender and golden.
4 Serve sliced pork with sauce, apple and onions.

prep & cook time 2 hours **serves** 6
nutritional count per serving 28.8g total fat (16.8g saturated fat); 2391kJ (572 cal); 14.7g carbohydrate; 55.1g protein; 3.8g fibre

roast loin of pork with apple sauce

Ask your butcher to roll and tie the pork at 2cm intervals for you, and to score the rind, if it isn't already done so.

2 sprigs rosemary
2.5kg boneless loin of pork, rind on
1 tablespoon olive oil
1 tablespoon coarse cooking salt
apple sauce
3 large apples (600g)
¼ cup (60ml) water
1 teaspoon white sugar
pinch ground cinnamon

1 Preheat oven to 250°C/230°C fan-forced.
2 Tuck the rosemary into the string under the pork. Place pork in large baking dish; rub rind with oil then salt. Roast about 40 minutes or until rind blisters. Drain excess fat from dish.
3 Reduce oven to 180°C/160°C fan-forced. Roast pork about 1 hour.
4 Meanwhile, make apple sauce.
5 Transfer pork to plate; cover loosely, stand 15 minutes before carving. Serve pork with apple sauce.
apple sauce Peel and core apples; slice thickly. Place apple and the water in medium saucepan; simmer, covered, 5 minutes. Uncover; simmer, further 5 minutes or until apple is soft. Remove from heat, stir in sugar and cinnamon.

prep & cook time 2 hours **serves** 8
nutritional count per serving 72g total fat (24.1g saturated fat); 3762kJ (900 cal); 7.7g carbohydrate; 56.7g protein; 1.1g fibre

pot-roasted pork with apple and sage

roast loin of pork with apple sauce

tip Broad beans can be bought ready-peeled and frozen just about as easily as peas and in this mash you won't be able to tell the difference between frozen and fresh ones. They also get the thumbs up from nutritionists as they are high in fibre and a good source of vitamin C and folate.

rhubarb and pear sponge pudding

825g can pear slices in natural juice
800g rhubarb, trimmed, cut into 4cm pieces
2 tablespoons caster sugar
2 eggs
⅓ cup (75g) caster sugar, extra
2 tablespoons plain flour
2 tablespoons self-raising flour
2 tablespoons cornflour

1 Preheat oven to 180°C/160°C fan-forced.
2 Drain pears; reserve ¾ cup (180ml) of the juice.
3 Place reserved juice, rhubarb and sugar in large saucepan; cook, stirring occasionally, about 5 minutes or until rhubarb is just tender. Stir in pears. Pour mixture into deep 1.75-litre (7-cup) ovenproof dish.
4 Meanwhile, beat eggs in small bowl with electric mixer until thick and creamy. Gradually add extra sugar, 1 tablespoon at a time, beating until sugar dissolves between additions. Gently fold in combined sifted flours.
5 Spread sponge mixture over hot rhubarb mixture. Bake about 45 minutes or until browned lightly and cooked through.

prep & cook time 1 hour 10 minutes **serves** 6
nutritional count per serving 2.1g total fat (0.6g saturated fat); 823kJ (197 cal); 35.7g carbohydrate; 5.4g protein; 5.9g fibre

lemon delicious pudding

125g butter, melted
2 teaspoons finely grated lemon rind
1½ cups (330g) caster sugar
3 eggs, separated
½ cup (75g) self-raising flour
⅓ cup (80ml) lemon juice
1⅓ cups (330ml) milk

1 Preheat oven to 180°C/160°C fan-forced. Grease six 1-cup (250ml) ovenproof dishes; place in large baking dish.
2 Combine butter, rind, sugar and yolks in large bowl. Whisk in sifted flour then juice. Gradually whisk in milk; mixture should be smooth and runny.
3 Beat egg whites in small bowl with electric mixer until soft peaks form; fold into lemon mixture in two batches.
4 Divide lemon mixture among dishes. Add enough boiling water to baking dish to come halfway up side of ovenproof dishes. Bake about 30 minutes or until puddings have risen and are a light golden colour.

prep & cook time 1 hour **serves** 6
nutritional count per serving 22g total fat (13.5g saturated fat); 2069kJ (495 cal); 67.1g carbohydrate; 6.7g protein; 0.5g fibre

apple, date and orange pie

8 medium Granny Smith apples (1.2kg),
  peeled, cored, sliced thickly
½ cup (125ml) water
1½ cups (210g) coarsely chopped dried dates
¼ cup (55g) caster sugar
2 teaspoons finely grated orange rind
1 tablespoon demerara sugar
pastry
1 cup (150g) plain flour
½ cup (75g) self-raising flour
¼ cup (35g) cornflour
¼ cup (30g) custard powder
1 tablespoon caster sugar
100g cold butter, chopped
1 egg, separated
¼ cup (60ml) cold water

1 Make pastry.
2 Place apples with the water in large saucepan; bring to the boil. Reduce heat; simmer, covered, 5 minutes. Add dates; simmer a further 5 minutes. Drain; stir in caster sugar and rind. Cool.
3 Preheat oven to 220°C/200°C fan-forced. Grease deep 25cm pie dish.
4 Divide pastry in half. Roll one half between sheets of baking paper until large enough to line dish. Spoon apple mixture into dish; brush pastry edges with egg white.
5 Roll remaining pastry large enough to cover filling. Press edges together. Brush pastry with egg white; sprinkle with demerara sugar. Bake 20 minutes. Reduce oven to 180°C/160°C fan-forced; bake a further 25 minutes.

pastry Process dry ingredients and butter until crumbly. Add egg yolk and the water; process until combined. Knead on floured surface until smooth. Cover; refrigerate 30 minutes.

prep & cook time 1 hour 50 minutes (+ refrigeration)
serves 8
nutritional count per serving 11.5g total fat (7g saturated fat); 1680kJ (402 cal); 68.5g carbohydrate; 4.9g protein; 5.7g fibre

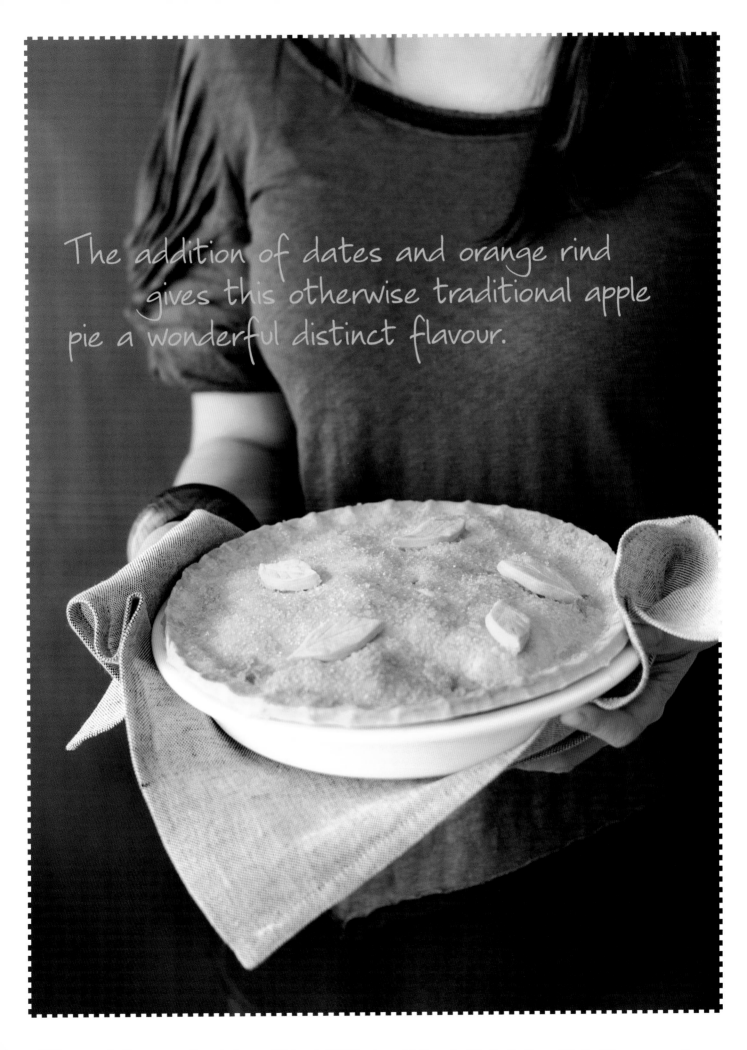

The addition of dates and orange rind gives this otherwise traditional apple pie a wonderful distinct flavour.

It's Friday night. Put a DVD on, sink into the couch and put your feet up.

classic fish and chips

lamb and tomato pide

classic fish and chips

1 cup (150g) self-raising flour
1 cup (250ml) dry ale
1 tablespoon sea salt
1kg potatoes, peeled
peanut oil, for deep-frying
4 x 150g blue-eye fillets, halved lengthways
tartare sauce
⅔ cup (200g) whole-egg mayonnaise
½ small brown onion (40g), chopped finely
2 tablespoons finely chopped cornichons
1 tablespoon drained, rinsed capers,
  chopped finely
1 tablespoon finely chopped fresh flat-leaf parsley
1 tablespoon lemon juice

1 Make tartare sauce.
2 Sift flour into medium bowl; whisk in beer and salt until smooth.
3 Cut potatoes lengthways into 1cm slices; cut each slice lengthways into 1cm-chips; dry with absorbent paper.
4 Heat oil in large saucepan. Cook chips, in three batches, about 2 minutes or until tender but not brown. Drain on absorbent paper.
5 Dip fish in batter; drain away excess. Deep-fry fish, in batches, until cooked. Drain on absorbent paper.
6 Deep-fry chips, in three batches, until crisp and golden brown; drain on absorbent paper.
7 Serve fish and chips with sauce and lemon wedges.
tartare sauce Combine ingredients in medium bowl.

prep & cook time 30 minutes **serves** 4
nutritional count per serving 38.3g total fat (6.2g saturated fat); 3340kJ (799 cal); 66.1g carbohydrate; 40.3g protein; 5.4g fibre

lamb and tomato pide

1 tablespoon olive oil
1 medium brown onion (150g), chopped finely
1 clove garlic, crushed
300g lamb mince
1 teaspoon ground cinnamon
1 teaspoon cumin
1 teaspoon smoked paprika
½ teaspoon cayenne pepper
1 tablespoon chopped fresh coriander
1 large tomato (220g), chopped coarsely
pizza dough
7g yeast
1 teaspoon sugar
⅔ cup (160ml) warm water
2 tablespoons warm milk
2 cups (300g) plain flour
1 teaspoon salt
1 tablespoon olive oil

1 Make pizza dough.
2 Preheat oven to 240°C/220°C fan-forced.
3 Heat oil in pan; cook onion and garlic until soft. Add lamb mince and spices; cook until lamb is browned. Stir in coriander; cool.
4 Divide dough into three; roll each piece to 12cm x 30cm. Spread filling across centre of each piece, leaving 2cm border. Brush edges with water; fold and press around dough. Fold corners to make oval shape.
5 Heat oven trays 3 minutes, place pide on trays; bake 10 minutes. Sprinkle with tomato; bake 5 minutes.
pizza dough Combine yeast, sugar, warm water and warm milk in jug. Stand in warm place until frothy. Place ½ cup of the flour in bowl; whisk in yeast mixture. Cover; stand in warm place 1 hour. Stir remaining flour, salt and oil into yeast mixture. Knead dough on floured surface until smooth. Place in oiled bowl, cover; stand in warm place 1 hour.

prep & cook time 1 hour (+ standing) **serves** 8
nutritional count per serving 10.5g total fat (2.4g saturated fat); 1087kJ (260 cal); 27.5g carbohydrate; 12.6g protein; 2.2g fibre

tip You could easily turn these patties into burgers if you wanted to. When you shape them into patties just make them a little wider and flatter than if you were serving them on their own.

These chicken patties are packed full of flavour and effortless to make.

chicken, tomato and fetta patties with spinach salad

750g chicken mince

⅓ cup (50g) drained semi-dried tomatoes, chopped coarsely

1 egg

½ cup (35g) stale breadcrumbs

200g fetta cheese, crumbled

1 small white onion (80g), sliced thinly

100g baby spinach leaves

1 tablespoon olive oil

1 tablespoon balsamic vinegar

1 Combine chicken, tomato, egg, breadcrumbs and half the cheese in large bowl; shape mixture into 12 patties.

2 Cook patties in heated oiled large frying pan, in batches, until cooked through. Drain on absorbent paper.

3 Meanwhile, combine onion, spinach, oil, vinegar and remaining cheese in medium bowl.

4 Serve patties with spinach salad.

prep & cook time 30 minutes **serves** 4
nutritional count per serving 33.7g total fat (13.3g saturated fat); 2320kJ (555 cal); 11.8g carbohydrate; 50.1g protein; 3.2g fibre

fajitas with guacamole

chinese barbecued spare ribs

barbecues

Marinate the meat, toss the salad and turn up the heat.

You can't get much more traditionally Turkish than this combination of lamb, spinach and fetta, but for a diversion from tradition try cooking these in a sandwich press — it works beautifully.

gözleme

4 cups (600g) plain flour
1 teaspoon coarse cooking salt
1⅔ cups (410ml) warm water
2 tablespoons vegetable oil
lamb filling
1 tablespoon vegetable oil
2 teaspoons ground cumin
½ teaspoon hot paprika
3 cloves garlic, crushed
500g lamb mince
400g can diced tomatoes
½ cup coarsely chopped fresh flat-leaf parsley
spinach and cheese filling
300g spinach, trimmed, shredded finely
½ cup coarsely chopped fresh mint
1 small brown onion (80g), chopped finely
½ teaspoon ground allspice
250g fetta cheese, crumbled
1 cup (100g) coarsely grated mozzarella cheese

1 Combine flour and salt in large bowl. Gradually stir in the water; mix to a soft dough. Knead dough on floured surface about 5 minutes or until smooth and elastic. Return to bowl; cover.
2 Make lamb filling.
3 Make spinach and cheese filling.
4 Divide dough into six pieces; roll each piece into 30cm square. Divide spinach and cheese filling among dough squares, spreading filling across centre of squares; top each with equal amounts of lamb filling. Fold top and bottom edges of dough over filling; tuck in ends to enclose.
5 Cook gözleme, both sides, over low heat on oiled grill plate, brushing with oil, until browned lightly and heated through.
lamb filling Heat oil in large frying pan; cook spices and garlic until fragrant. Add lamb; cook, stirring, until browned. Add undrained tomatoes; simmer about 15 minutes or until liquid is almost evaporated. Stir in parsley.
spinach and cheese filling Combine ingredients in medium bowl.

prep & cook time 1 hour **serves** 6
nutritional count per serving 29.9g total fat (12.7g saturated fat); 3168kJ (758 cal); 75.8g carbohydrate; 41.8g protein; 7.1g fibre

barbecued lamb, shallot and mesclun salad

150g sugar snap peas, trimmed
600g lamb backstrap
8 large shallots (200g), peeled, quartered
60g mesclun
mint dressing
1 cup firmly packed fresh mint leaves
2 cloves garlic, quartered
¼ cup (60ml) olive oil
2 tablespoons white wine vinegar
2 teaspoons caster sugar

1 Boil, steam or microwave peas until tender; drain.
2 Meanwhile, cook lamb and shallots on heated oiled grill plate (or grill or barbecue) until lamb is cooked as desired and shallots are tender. Cover lamb; stand 5 minutes then slice thinly.
3 Make mint dressing.
4 Combine peas, lamb, shallot, dressing and mesclun in large bowl.
mint dressing Blend or process mint and garlic until smooth. With motor operating, gradually add oil in a thin, steady stream; blend until smooth. Stir in vinegar and sugar.

prep & cook time 25 minutes **serves** 4
nutritional count per serving 19.4g total fat (4.4g saturated fat); 1404kJ (336 cal); 6.2g carbohydrate; 33.2g protein; 2.7g fibre

lamb kebabs

Soak 12 bamboo skewers in water for at least an hour before using to prevent them from scorching during cooking.

500g lamb mince
1 egg
1 small brown onion (80g), chopped finely
2 tablespoons finely chopped fresh flat-leaf parsley
1 clove garlic, crushed
2 teaspoons ground cinnamon
2 teaspoons sweet paprika
½ teaspoon cayenne pepper
½ cup (120g) greek-style yogurt

1 Combine ingredients in large bowl.
2 Form lamb mixture into 16 sausage shapes, thread onto 16 small bamboo skewers or strong toothpicks; flatten slightly.
3 Cook skewers on heated oiled grill plate (or grill or barbecue) until browned and cooked as desired. Serve with yogurt, lemon wedges and pitta bread.

prep & cook time 30 minutes **serves** 4
nutritional count per serving 10.8g total fat (4.8g saturated fat); 1004kJ (240 cal); 5.6g carbohydrate; 29.2g protein; 0.4g fibre

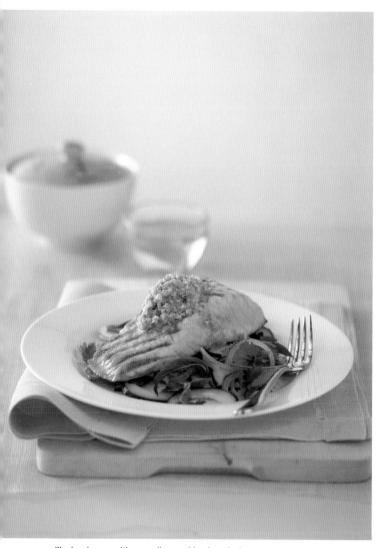

grilled salmon with nam jim and herb salad

barbecued baby octopus

grilled salmon with nam jim and herb salad

4 x 220g salmon fillets, skin-on
nam jim
3 long green chillies, chopped coarsely
2 fresh small red thai chillies, chopped coarsely
2 cloves garlic, quartered
1 shallot (25g), quartered
2cm piece fresh ginger (10g), quartered
⅓ cup (80ml) lime juice
2 tablespoons fish sauce
1 tablespoon grated palm sugar
1 tablespoon peanut oil
¼ cup (35g) roasted unsalted cashews,
   chopped finely
herb salad
1½ cups loosely packed fresh mint leaves
1 cup loosely packed fresh coriander leaves
1 cup loosely packed fresh basil leaves, torn
1 medium red onion (170g), sliced thinly
2 lebanese cucumbers (260g), seeded, sliced thinly

1 Make nam jim.
2 Cook salmon, both sides, on heated oiled grill plate (or grill or barbecue) until cooked as desired.
3 Meanwhile, make herb salad.
4 Serve salmon and herb salad topped with nam jim.
nam jim Blend or process chillies, garlic, shallot, ginger, juice, sauce, sugar and oil until smooth; stir in nuts.
herb salad Place ingredients in medium bowl; toss gently to combine.

prep & cook time 40 minutes **serves** 4
nutritional count per serving 25g total fat (5.1g saturated fat); 1948kJ (466 cal); 10.8g carbohydrate; 47.6g protein; 4.4g fibre

barbecued baby octopus

1kg baby octopus
⅓ cup (80ml) lemon juice
⅓ cup (80ml) olive oil
2 cloves garlic, crushed
2 teaspoons dried rigani
1 medium lemon, cut into wedges

1 Clean octopus, remove eyes and beaks. Combine octopus with juice, oil, garlic and rigani in medium bowl. Cover, refrigerate 3 hours or overnight.
2 Drain octopus; discard marinade. Cook octopus on heated oiled barbecue (or grill or grill plate) until tender. Serve with lemon wedges.

prep & cook time 25 minutes (+ refrigeration)
serves 6
nutritional count per serving 13.4g total fat (1.7g saturated fat); 982kJ (235 cal); 1g carbohydrate; 27.6g protein; 0.2g fibre
tip Rigani is a Greek oregano; it is a stronger, sharper version of the familiar herb we use in Italian cooking and is available from good delicatessens and Mediterranean food stores.

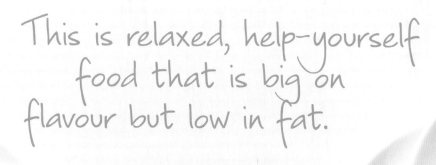

This is relaxed, help-yourself food that is big on flavour but low in fat.

barbecued seafood platter

16 uncooked medium king prawns (720g)
1 teaspoon finely grated lemon rind
½ teaspoon dried chilli flakes
1 clove garlic, crushed
1 tablespoon finely chopped fresh oregano
2 tablespoons olive oil
8 slices prosciutto (120g)
8 butterflied sardines (240g)
300g baby octopus, quartered
200g squid hoods, sliced into rings
2 tablespoons balsamic vinegar
¼ cup coarsely chopped fresh flat-leaf parsley
500g small black mussels
¼ cup (60ml) lemon juice
1 medium tomato (150g), seeded, chopped finely

1 Remove and discard prawn heads. Cut prawns lengthwise, three-quarters of the way through, (and down to 1cm before the tail) leaving shells intact; press down on prawns on board to flatten.
2 Combine prawns, rind, chilli, garlic, oregano and half the oil in medium bowl; cover, refrigerate 1 hour.
3 Wrap a prosciutto slice firmly around each sardine.
4 Cook octopus and squid on heated oiled grill plate (or grill or barbecue). Combine octopus and squid in medium heatproof bowl with remaining oil, vinegar and 2 tablespoons of the parsley. Cover to keep warm.
5 Cook prawns and sardines on heated oiled grill plate (or grill or barbecue).
6 Meanwhile, cook mussels, covered, on heated oiled flat plate about 5 minutes or until mussels open (discard any that do not). Place mussels in medium heatproof bowl; drizzle with juice, sprinkle with tomato and remaining parsley.
7 Serve seafood with lemon wedges.

prep & cook time 1 hour (+ refrigeration) **serves** 8
nutritional count per serving 8.7g total fat (1.7g saturated fat); 836kJ (200 cal); 1.3g carbohydrate; 28.5g protein; 0.4g fibre

grilled balmain bug salad

plum and star anise pork spare ribs

grilled balmain bug salad

2 baby eggplants (120g)
1 medium zucchini (120g)
1 medium red capsicum (200g), chopped finely
3 flat mushrooms (240g), quartered
2 tablespoons olive oil
6 uncooked balmain bug tails (1.5kg),
    halved lengthways
250g rocket, trimmed
chilli lime butter
60g butter, softened
2 teaspoons finely grated lime rind
2 tablespoons lime juice
1 fresh long red chilli, chopped finely
2 cloves garlic, crushed

1 Using vegetable peeler, cut eggplant and zucchini into long, thin strips. Combine eggplant, zucchini, capsicum, mushrooms and oil in large bowl.
2 Cook vegetables, in batches, on heated oiled grill plate (or grill or barbecue) until tender. Cover to keep warm.
3 Cook balmain bug on heated oiled grill plate until cooked.
4 Meanwhile, make chilli lime butter.
5 Combine vegetables, balmain bug and chilli lime butter in large bowl.
6 Divide rocket among serving plates; top with vegetable and balmain bug mixture.
chilli lime butter Combine ingredients in small bowl.

prep & cook time 40 minutes **serves** 4
nutritional count per serving 25.1g total fat (10g saturated fat); 2282kJ (456 cal); 5.4g carbohydrate; 72.4g protein; 4.6g fibre

plum and star anise pork spare ribs

2kg slabs american-style pork spare ribs
plum and star anise marinade
1 cup (250ml) plum sauce
5cm piece fresh ginger (25g), grated
⅓ cup (80ml) oyster sauce
2 star anise
1 teaspoon dried chilli flakes
pear, ginger and chilli salad
2 medium pears (460g), sliced thinly
2 fresh long red chillies, sliced thinly
2 green onions, sliced thinly
2 cups coarsely chopped fresh mint
2cm piece fresh ginger (10g), grated
2 tablespoons lime juice

1 Make plum and star anise marinade.
2 Place pork in large shallow baking dish; brush marinade all over pork. Pour remaining marinade over pork; cover, refrigerate 3 hours or overnight, turning pork occasionally.
3 Drain pork; reserve marinade. Cook pork on heated oiled grill plate (or grill or barbecue) about 30 minutes or until cooked through, turning and brushing frequently with some of the reserved marinade.
4 Meanwhile, make pear, ginger and chilli salad.
5 Boil remaining marinade, uncovered, in small saucepan about 5 minutes or until thickened slightly.
6 Slice slabs into portions; serve with hot marinade and salad.
plum and star anise marinade Bring ingredients to the boil in medium saucepan. Remove from heat; cool 10 minutes.
pear, ginger and chilli salad Combine ingredients in medium bowl.

prep & cook time 55 minutes (+ refrigeration)
serves 4
nutritional count per serving 18.1g total fat (6.6g saturated fat); 2847kJ (681 cal); 56.3g carbohydrate; 69.6g protein; 5.2g fibre

grilled pork sausages with fruit relish

1 tablespoon olive oil
1 small red onion (100g), chopped finely
1 clove garlic, crushed
2 medium pears (460g), chopped finely
¼ cup (55g) finely chopped dried apricots
¼ cup (40g) sultanas, chopped finely
2 tablespoons cider vinegar
2 tablespoons brown sugar
½ teaspoon ground allspice
12 thick pork sausages (1.5kg)

1 Heat oil in medium saucepan; cook onion and garlic, stirring, until onions soften. Add fruit, vinegar, sugar and spice; cook, uncovered, stirring occasionally, about 10 minutes or until mixture is thick and pulpy.
2 Meanwhile, cook sausages on heated oiled grill plate (or grill or barbecue) until cooked through.
3 Serve sausages with fruit relish.

prep & cook time 30 minutes **serves** 6
nutritional count per serving 58.7g total fat (22.9g saturated fat); 3252kJ (778 cal); 29.9g carbohydrate; 31g protein; 6.2g fibre

spiced sliced rump with chilli peanut sauce

1 fresh small red thai chilli, chopped finely
1 shallot (25g), chopped finely
1 tablespoon peanut oil
800g beef rump steak
¼ cup (60ml) water
⅓ cup (75g) caster sugar
¼ cup (60ml) fish sauce
½ cup (125ml) lime juice
1 medium carrot (120g), chopped finely
1 medium red capsicum (200g), chopped finely
1 cup (140g) crushed roasted unsalted peanuts
20 peking duck pancakes (200g)

1 Combine chilli and shallot in medium bowl. Combine half the chilli mixture with oil in large bowl; add beef, turn to coat in mixture.
2 Cook beef on heated oiled flat plate (or grill or barbecue), turning once, until cooked. Cover; stand 5 minutes, slice thinly.
3 Meanwhile, stir the water, sugar, sauce, juice, carrot, capsicum and nuts into remaining chilli mixture.
4 Heat pancakes by folding each into quarters; place in steamer over large saucepan of simmering water until just pliable. Serve beef with chilli peanut sauce and pancakes.

prep & cook time 45 minutes **serves** 4
nutritional count per serving 35.6g total fat (9.4g saturated fat); 3047kJ (729 cal); 41.1g carbohydrate; 58.6g protein; 5.4g fibre

from grandma's kitchen

Take yourself back in time with these old-fashioned classic recipes.

This old favourite is pure comfort food in a bowl — it's just the thing to relieve winter chills.

cream of chicken soup

2 litres (8 cups) water
1 litre (4 cups) chicken stock
1.8kg whole chicken
1 medium carrot (120g), chopped coarsely
1 stalk celery (150g), trimmed, chopped coarsely
1 medium brown onion (150g), chopped coarsely
40g butter
⅓ cup (50g) plain flour
2 tablespoons lemon juice
½ cup (125ml) cream
¼ cup finely chopped fresh flat-leaf parsley

1 Place the water and stock in large saucepan with chicken, carrot, celery and onion; bring to the boil. Reduce heat; simmer, covered, 1½ hours. Remove chicken from pan; simmer broth, covered, 30 minutes.
2 Strain broth through muslin-lined sieve or colander into large heatproof bowl; discard solids.
3 Melt butter in large saucepan, add flour; cook, stirring, until mixture thickens and bubbles. Gradually stir in broth and juice; stir over heat until mixture boils and thickens slightly. Add cream, reduce heat; simmer, uncovered, about 25 minutes, stirring occasionally.
4 Meanwhile, remove and discard skin and bones from chicken; shred meat coarsely. Add chicken to soup; stir over medium heat until hot.
5 Sprinkle soup with parsley; serve with crusty bread, if you like.

prep & cook time 3 hours **serves** 4
nutritional count per serving 59.2g total fat (26.2g saturated fat); 3327kJ (796 cal); 15.7g carbohydrate; 50.7g protein; 2.5g fibre

irish stew

rabbit stew

serving idea If you've got some little baking dishes you could make this pie in individual servings and present each diner with their own dish. You can also make this recipe with cooked lamb mince if you prefer.

apple pie

10 medium apples (1.5kg)
½ cup (125ml) water
¼ cup (55g) caster sugar
1 teaspoon finely grated lemon rind
¼ teaspoon ground cinnamon
1 egg white
1 tablespoon caster sugar, extra
pastry
1 cup (150g) plain flour
½ cup (75g) self-raising flour
¼ cup (35g) cornflour
¼ cup (30g) custard powder
1 tablespoon caster sugar
100g cold butter, chopped coarsely
1 egg yolk
¼ cup (60ml) iced water

1 Make pastry.

2 Peel, core and slice apple thickly. Place apples and the water in large saucepan; bring to the boil. Reduce heat; simmer, covered, about 10 minutes or until apples soften. Drain; stir in sugar, rind and cinnamon. Cool.

3 Preheat oven to 220°C/200°C fan-forced. Grease deep 25cm pie dish.

4 Divide pastry in half. Roll one half between sheets of baking paper until large enough to line dish. Lift pastry into dish; press into base and side. Spoon apple mixture into pastry case; brush edge with egg white.

5 Roll remaining pastry large enough to cover filling; lift onto filling. Press edges together; trim away excess pastry. Brush pastry with egg white; sprinkle with extra sugar. Bake 20 minutes.

6 Reduce oven to 180°C/160°C fan-forced; bake pie a further 25 minutes or until golden brown. Serve with vanilla custard or ice-cream.

pastry Process dry ingredients with the butter until crumbly. Add egg yolk and the water; process until combined. Knead on floured surface until smooth. Cover; refrigerate 30 minutes.

prep + cook time 1 hour 45 minutes (+ refrigeration)
serves 8
nutritional count per serving 11.4g total fat (7g saturated fat); 1438kJ (344 cal); 53.9g carbohydrate; 4.3g protein; 3.7g fibre

tip Golden Delicious apples are the best variety to bake with as they hold their shape well and develop a lovely mellow, sweet flavour when cooked.

classic trifle

pavlova

classic trifle

85g packet raspberry jelly crystals
250g sponge cake, cut into 3cm pieces
¼ cup (60ml) sweet sherry
¼ cup (30g) custard powder
¼ cup (55g) caster sugar
½ teaspoon vanilla extract
1½ cups (375ml) milk
825g can sliced peaches, drained
300ml thickened cream
2 tablespoons flaked almonds, roasted

1 Make jelly according to directions on packet;
pour into shallow container. Refrigerate 20 minutes or
until jelly is almost set.
2 Arrange cake in 3-litre (12-cup) bowl; sprinkle
with sherry.
3 Blend custard powder, sugar and extract with a
little of the milk in small saucepan; stir in remaining
milk. Stir over heat until mixture boils and thickens.
Cover surface with plastic wrap; cool.
4 Pour jelly over cake; refrigerate 15 minutes. Top
with peaches. Stir a third of the cream into custard;
pour over peaches.
5 Whip remaining cream; spread over custard,
sprinkle with nuts. Refrigerate 3 hours or overnight.

prep & cook time 40 minutes (+ refrigeration)
serves 8
nutritional count per serving 18.3g total fat (10.7g
saturated fat); 1643kJ (393 cal); 49g carbohydrate;
6.9g protein; 2.1g fibre

pavlova

4 egg whites
1 cup (220g) caster sugar
½ teaspoon vanilla extract
¾ teaspoon white vinegar
300ml thickened cream, whipped
250g strawberries, halved
¼ cup (60ml) passionfruit pulp

1 Preheat oven to 120°C/100°C fan-forced. Line
oven tray with foil; grease foil, dust with cornflour,
shake away excess. Mark 18cm-circle on foil.
2 Beat egg whites in small bowl with electric mixer
until soft peaks form; gradually add sugar, beating
until sugar dissolves. Add extract and vinegar; beat
until combined.
3 Spread meringue into circle on foil, building up at
the side to 8cm in height. Smooth side and top of
pavlova gently. Using spatula blade, mark decorative
grooves around side of pavlova; smooth top again.
4 Bake pavlova about 1½ hours. Turn oven off; cool
pavlova in oven with door ajar.
5 Cut around top edge of pavlova (the crisp meringue
top will fall on top of the marshmallow centre). Serve
pavlova topped with whipped cream, strawberries
and passionfruit.

prep & cook time 1 hour 50 minutes (+ cooling)
serves 8
nutritional count per serving 14g total fat (9.2g
saturated fat); 1095kJ (262 cal); 30g carbohydrate;
3.3g protein; 1.7g fibre

scones

4 cups (600g) self-raising flour
2 tablespoons icing sugar
60g butter
1½ cups (375ml) milk
¾ cup (180ml) water, approximately

1 Preheat oven to 220°C/ 200°C fan-forced. Grease 20cm x 30cm lamington pan.
2 Sift flour and sugar into large bowl; rub in butter with fingertips.
3 Make a well in centre of flour mixture; add milk and almost all the water. Use knife to "cut" the milk and water through the flour mixture, mixing to a soft, sticky dough. Knead dough on floured surface until smooth.

4 Press dough out to 2cm thickness. Dip 4.5cm round cutter in flour; cut as many rounds as you can from piece of dough. Place scones, side by side, just touching, in pan.
5 Gently knead scraps of dough together; repeat pressing and cutting of dough, place in same pan. Brush tops with a little extra milk; bake 15 minutes or until scones are just browned and sound hollow when tapped firmly on the top with fingers.

prep & cook time 45 minutes **makes** 20
nutritional count per scone 3.6g total fat (2.2g saturated fat); 606kJ (145 cal); 23.6g carbohydrate; 3.9g protein; 1.1g fibre

serving idea Try substituting brioche or croissants instead of sliced bread for an even more luxurious version of this classic dessert. Berries, especially raspberries, also make a delicious addition.

One of the most comforting puddings, it has just the right amount of custard to soak through its layers of bread.

bread and butter pudding

6 slices white bread (270g)
40g butter, softened
½ cup (80g) sultanas
¼ teaspoon ground nutmeg
custard
1½ cups (375ml) milk
2 cups (500ml) cream
⅓ cup (75g) caster sugar
1 teaspoon vanilla extract
4 eggs

1 Preheat oven to 160°C/140°C fan-forced. Grease shallow 2-litre (8-cup) ovenproof dish.
2 Make custard.
3 Trim crusts from bread. Spread each slice with butter; cut into four triangles. Layer bread, overlapping, in dish; sprinkle with sultanas. Pour custard over bread; sprinkle with nutmeg.
4 Place ovenproof dish in large baking dish; add enough boiling water to come halfway up side of ovenproof dish. Bake about 45 minutes or until pudding is set. Remove pudding from baking dish; stand 5 minutes before serving. Serve dusted with sifted icing sugar.
custard Bring milk, cream, sugar and extract to the boil in medium saucepan. Whisk eggs in large bowl; whisking constantly, gradually add hot milk mixture to egg mixture.

prep & cook time 1 hour 15 minutes **serves** 6
nutritional count per serving 48.6g total fat (30.4g saturated fat); 2859kJ (684 cal); 49.3g carbohydrate; 12.4g protein; 1.8g fibre

hedgehog slice

¾ cup (180ml) sweetened condensed milk
60g butter
125g dark eating chocolate, chopped coarsely
150g plain sweet biscuits
⅓ cup (45g) roasted unsalted peanuts
⅓ cup (55g) sultanas

1 Grease 8cm x 26cm bar pan; line base with baking paper, extending paper 5cm over long sides.
2 Combine condensed milk and butter in small saucepan; stir over low heat until smooth. Remove from heat; add chocolate, stir until smooth.
3 Break biscuits into small pieces; place in large bowl with nuts and sultanas. Add chocolate mixture; stir to combine.
4 Spread mixture into pan; cover, refrigerate 4 hours or until firm. Remove from pan; cut into slices.

prep & cook time 20 minutes (+ refrigeration)
makes 12
nutritional count per slice 12.7g total fat (6.8g saturated fat); 1028kJ (246 cal); 29.9g carbohydrate; 4g protein; 0.9g fibre

kisses

125g butter, softened
½ cup (110g) caster sugar
1 egg
⅓ cup (50g) plain flour
¼ cup (35g) self-raising flour
⅔ cup (100g) cornflour
¼ cup (30g) custard powder
vienna cream
60g butter, softened
¾ cup (120g) icing sugar
2 teaspoons milk

1 Preheat oven to 180°C/160°C fan-forced. Grease two oven trays.
2 Beat butter and sugar in small bowl with electric mixer until smooth and creamy; beat in egg. Stir in sifted dry ingredients in two batches.
3 Spoon mixture into piping bag fitted with 1cm tube. Pipe 3cm-diameter rounds of mixture, about 3cm apart, onto trays. Bake about 10 minutes or until browned lightly. Loosen cakes; cool on trays.
4 Meanwhile, make vienna cream.
5 Sandwich cold cakes with vienna cream; dust with a little extra sifted icing sugar.
vienna cream Beat butter until as white as possible. Gradually beat in half the sifted icing sugar; beat in milk. Gradually beat in remaining icing sugar.

prep & cook time 40 minutes **makes about** 40
nutritional count per kiss 4g total fat (2.6g saturated fat); 322kJ (77 cal); 10g carbohydrate; 0.5g protein; 0.1g fibre

world food

Let these exotic flavours from around the world seduce you to the table.

This traditional Spanish dish varies from region to region, and each one claims theirs as the best and most authentic.

paella

500g clams
1 tablespoon coarse cooking salt
500g uncooked medium prawns
500g small black mussels
2 tablespoons olive oil
3 cups (750ml) chicken stock
pinch saffron threads
220g chicken thigh fillets, chopped coarsely
1 chorizo sausage (170g), sliced thickly
1 large red onion (300g), chopped finely
1 medium red capsicum (200g), chopped finely
2 cloves garlic, crushed
2 teaspoons smoked paprika
2 medium tomatoes (300g), peeled, seeded,
    chopped finely
1½ cups (300g) calasparra rice
1 cup (120g) frozen peas
2 tablespoons finely chopped fresh flat-leaf parsley

1 Rinse clams under cold water, place in large bowl with salt; cover with cold water, stand 2 hours. Drain then rinse.
2 Shell and devein prawns, leaving tails intact. Reserve shells. Scrub mussels and remove beards.
3 Heat 2 teaspoons of the oil in large saucepan, add prawn shells; cook, stirring, until red. Add stock; bring to the boil. Reduce heat; simmer, uncovered, 20 minutes. Strain through fine sieve into jug or bowl; add saffron to the liquid. Discard prawn shells.
4 Heat another 2 teaspoons of the oil in 45cm paella pan or large frying pan, add chicken; cook until browned all over, remove from pan. Add chorizo to same pan; cook until browned all over. Remove chorizo from pan; drain on absorbent paper.
5 Heat remaining oil in pan, add onion, capsicum, garlic, paprika and tomato; cook, stirring, until soft. Add rice; stir to coat in mixture.
6 Add chicken, chorizo and stock to pan; stir until combined. Bring mixture to the boil; reduce heat, simmer, uncovered, about 15 minutes or until rice is almost tender.
7 Sprinkle peas over rice; place clams, prawns and mussels evenly over surface of paella. Cover pan with a lid or large sheets of foil; simmer about 5 minutes or until prawns are cooked and mussels and clams have opened (discard any that do not). Sprinkle with parsley; serve immediately.

prep & cook time 2 hours (+ standing) **serves** 6
nutritional count per serving 18.9g total fat (5.2g saturated fat); 2128kJ (509 cal); 49.1g carbohydrate; 33.6g protein; 3.7g fibre

tortilla de patata

20g butter
¼ cup (60ml) olive oil
3 medium potatoes (600g), chopped finely
1 medium brown onion (150g), chopped finely
8 eggs
½ teaspoon chilli powder

1 Preheat oven to 180°C/160°C fan-forced.
2 Melt butter with oil in 22cm-base ovenproof frying pan; cook potato and onion, stirring occasionally, until potato is tender.

3 Meanwhile, whisk eggs and chilli powder in medium jug.
4 Add egg mixture to pan. Cook, uncovered, over low heat, about 5 minutes or until just set.
5 Place pan in oven; cook, uncovered, 10 minutes or until browned lightly. Carefully turn tortilla onto plate. Cut into wedges; serve with a side salad.

prep & cook time 40 minutes **serves** 4
nutritional count per serving 28.4g total fat (7.8g saturated fat); 1747kJ (418 cal); 22g carbohydrate; 17.5g protein; 28.4g fibre

serving idea This risotto looks so
appealing in a large saucepan,
especially with some parsley sprinkled
on top, so bring the whole pan to the
table and dish it up from there.

mushroom fettuccine boscaiola

spinach and herb cannelloni

mushroom fettuccine boscaiola

10g dried porcini mushrooms
¼ cup (60ml) boiling water
375g fettuccine
1 tablespoon olive oil
200g pancetta, chopped coarsely
100g button mushrooms, sliced thinly
100g swiss brown mushrooms, sliced thinly
1 flat mushroom (80g), sliced thinly
2 cloves garlic, crushed
¼ cup (60ml) dry white wine
300ml cream
1 tablespoon lemon juice
½ cup (40g) finely grated parmesan cheese
2 tablespoons coarsely chopped fresh chives
2 tablespoons finely grated parmesan cheese, extra

1 Combine porcini mushrooms and the water in small heatproof bowl; cover, stand 15 minutes or until mushrooms are tender. Drain; reserve soaking liquid, chop mushrooms coarsely.
2 Cook pasta in large saucepan of boiling water until tender; drain.
3 Meanwhile, heat oil in large frying pan; cook pancetta until crisp. Add all mushrooms and garlic; cook, stirring, until mushrooms are browned lightly. Add wine; bring to the boil. Boil, uncovered, until liquid has almost evaporated. Add cream, juice and reserved soaking liquid; simmer, uncovered, until sauce reduces by half and thickens slightly. Stir in cheese and chives.
4 Combine pasta and sauce in large bowl. Serve bowls of pasta sprinkled with extra parmesan cheese.

prep & cook time 40 minutes (+ standing) **serves** 4
nutritional count per serving 45.5g total fat (26.1g saturated fat); 3390kJ (811 cal); 66.9g carbohydrate; 28.9g protein; 5.3g fibre

spinach and herb cannelloni

1kg spinach, trimmed, chopped coarsely
500g ricotta cheese
2 eggs
1½ cups (120g) coarsely grated parmesan cheese
¼ cup finely chopped fresh mint
3 teaspoons finely chopped fresh thyme
2 teaspoons finely chopped fresh rosemary
250g cannelloni tubes
creamy tomato sauce
1 tablespoon olive oil
1 medium brown onion (150g), chopped finely
4 cloves garlic, crushed
4 x 400g cans diced tomatoes
½ cup (125ml) cream
1 teaspoon white sugar

1 Make creamy tomato sauce.
2 Meanwhile, preheat oven to 180°C/160°C fan-forced.
3 Cook washed, drained (not dried) spinach in heated large saucepan, stirring, until wilted. Drain; when cool enough to handle, squeeze out excess moisture.
4 Combine spinach in large bowl with ricotta, eggs, ½ cup of the parmesan cheese and the herbs. Using a large piping bag, fill pasta with spinach mixture.
5 Spread a third of the sauce into shallow 25cm x 35cm ovenproof dish; top with pasta, in single layer, then top with remaining sauce. Cook, covered, in oven, 20 minutes. Uncover, sprinkle pasta with remaining parmesan; cook about 15 minutes or until pasta is tender and cheese is browned lightly.
creamy tomato sauce Heat oil in large saucepan; cook onion, stirring, until softened. Add garlic; cook, stirring, until fragrant. Add undrained tomatoes; bring to the boil. Reduce heat; simmer, uncovered, stirring occasionally, about 20 minutes or until sauce thickens slightly. Cool 10 minutes; blend or process sauce with cream and sugar until smooth.

prep & cook time 1 hour **serves** 6
nutritional count per serving 31g total fat (17.1g saturated fat); 2412kJ (577 cal); 41.8g carbohydrate; 28.7g protein; 8.3g fibre

Osso buco originates from Milan and is traditionally served on risotto alla milanese (saffron risotto) with a good sprinkle of gremolata. Here we've served it on polenta.

osso buco

6 pieces veal osso buco (1.8kg)
½ cup (75g) plain flour
40g butter
2 tablespoons olive oil
3 stalks celery (450g), trimmed, chopped coarsely
6 drained anchovy fillets, chopped coarsely
¾ cup (180ml) dry white wine
2 x 400g cans diced tomatoes
½ cup (125ml) chicken stock
5 cloves garlic, crushed
3 bay leaves
10 fresh thyme sprigs
gremolata
½ cup finely chopped fresh flat-leaf parsley
2 cloves garlic, chopped finely
1 teaspoon finely grated lemon rind

1 Preheat oven to 160°C/140°C fan-forced.
2 Coat veal in flour, shake off any excess. Heat butter and oil in large frying pan; cook veal, in batches, until browned both sides. Transfer veal to large ovenproof dish.
3 Cook celery and anchovy in same pan, stirring, until celery softens. Add wine; bring to the boil. Stir in undrained tomatoes, stock, garlic, bay leaves and thyme; return to the boil.
4 Pour tomato mixture over veal. Cook, covered, in oven about 1½ hours or until veal starts to fall from the bone.
5 Meanwhile, make gremolata.
6 Serve osso buco sprinkled with gremolata.
gremolata Combine ingredients in small bowl.

prep & cook time 2 hours **serves** 6
nutritional count per serving 13.2g total fat (4.8g saturated fat); 1626kJ (389 cal); 14.4g carbohydrate; 46.1g protein; 3.8g fibre

veal saltimbocca

chicken wonton soup

veal saltimbocca

8 veal schnitzels (800g)
8 slices prosciutto (120g)
4 bocconcini cheese (240g), sliced thinly
⅔ cup (100g) drained semi-dried tomatoes
16 fresh sage leaves
40g butter
1 cup (250ml) dry white wine
1 tablespoon lemon juice
2 tablespoons coarsely chopped fresh sage

1 Top each piece of veal with prosciutto, cheese, tomatoes and sage leaves. Fold in half to secure filling; secure with toothpicks or small skewers.
2 Melt half the butter in medium frying pan; cook veal, in batches, until cooked as desired. Cover to keep warm.
3 Add wine to same pan; bring to the boil. Boil, uncovered, until wine reduces by half. Stir in remaining butter, juice and sage.
4 Serve saltimbocca drizzled with sauce.

prep & cook time 35 minutes **serves** 4
nutritional count per serving 24g total fat (13.1g saturated fat); 2312kJ (553 cal); 9g carbohydrate; 63.3g protein; 3.6g fibre

chicken wonton soup

1 tablespoon olive oil
1 medium brown onion (150g), chopped coarsely
1 clove garlic, sliced thinly
2cm piece fresh ginger (10g), sliced thinly
1.5 litres (6 cups) water
2 cups (500ml) chicken stock
1kg chicken bones
1 medium carrot (120g), chopped coarsely
1 stalk celery (150g), trimmed, chopped coarsely
1 tablespoon light soy sauce
4 green onions, sliced thinly
chicken wontons
150g chicken mince
1 fresh small red thai chilli, chopped finely
1 clove garlic, crushed
1cm piece fresh ginger (5g), grated
2 teaspoons light soy sauce
1 green onion, sliced thinly
16 x 8cm round wonton wrappers

1 Heat oil in large saucepan; cook brown onion, garlic and ginger, stirring, until onion softens. Add the water, stock, bones, carrot and celery; bring to the boil. Reduce heat; simmer, covered, 2 hours.
2 Strain broth through muslin-lined sieve or colander into large heatproof bowl; discard solids. Cool; cover, refrigerate overnight.
3 Make chicken wontons.
4 Skim and discard fat from surface of broth. Return broth to large saucepan with sauce; bring to the boil. Add wontons, reduce heat; cook about 5 minutes.
5 Divide wontons among bowls; ladle broth into bowls and sprinkle with green onion.
chicken wontons Combine chicken, chilli, garlic, ginger, sauce and onion in small bowl. Place a rounded teaspoon of chicken mixture in centre of each wonton wrapper; brush around edges with a little water, gather edges around filling, pinch together to seal.

prep & cook time 3 hours (+ refrigeration) **serves** 4
nutritional count per serving 5.5g total fat (2g saturated fat); 560kJ (134 cal); 4.7g carbohydrate; 16.6g protein; 0.2g fibre

sang choy bow

2 teaspoons sesame oil
1 small brown onion (80g), chopped finely
2 cloves garlic, crushed
2cm piece fresh ginger (10g), grated
500g lean pork mince
2 tablespoons water
100g shiitake mushrooms, chopped finely
2 tablespoons light soy sauce
2 tablespoons oyster sauce
1 tablespoon lime juice
2 cups bean sprouts
4 green onions, sliced thinly
¼ cup coarsely chopped fresh coriander
12 large butter lettuce leaves

1 Heat oil in wok; stir-fry brown onion, garlic and ginger until onion softens. Add pork; stir-fry until changed in colour.
2 Add the water, mushrooms, sauces and juice; stir-fry until mushrooms are tender. Remove from heat. Add sprouts, green onion and coriander; toss to combine.
3 Spoon sang choy bow into lettuce leaves to serve.

prep & cook time 30 minutes **serves** 4
nutritional count per serving 11.5g total fat (3.6g saturated fat); 1112kJ (266 cal); 8.9g carbohydrate; 29.3g protein; 4.1g fibre

pho bo

2 litres (8 cups) water
1 litre (4 cups) beef stock
1kg beef chuck steak
2 star anise
8cm piece fresh ginger (40g), grated
⅓ cup (80ml) japanese soy sauce
200g bean thread noodles
1½ cups (120g) bean sprouts
¼ cup loosely packed fresh coriander leaves
⅓ cup loosely packed fresh mint leaves
4 green onions, sliced thinly
2 fresh long red chillies, sliced thinly
¼ cup (60ml) fish sauce
1 lime, cut into wedges

1 Place the water and stock in large saucepan with beef, star anise, ginger and soy sauce; bring to the boil. Reduce heat; simmer, covered, 30 minutes. Uncover; simmer about 30 minutes or until beef is tender.
2 Meanwhile, place noodles in medium heatproof bowl, cover with boiling water; stand until just tender, drain.
3 Combine sprouts, herbs, onion and chilli in medium bowl.
4 Remove beef from pan. Strain broth through muslin-lined sieve or colander into large heatproof bowl; discard solids. When beef is cool enough to handle, remove and discard fat and sinew. Slice beef thinly, return to same cleaned pan with broth; bring to the boil. Stir in fish sauce.
5 Divide noodles among soup bowls; ladle hot beef broth into bowls, sprinkle with sprout mixture and serve with lime wedges.

prep & cook time 1 hour 40 minutes **serves** 6
nutritional count per serving 13.8g total fat (6.2g saturated fat); 1601kJ (383 cal); 21g carbohydrate; 41.3g protein; 4.1g fibre

sang choy bow

pho bo

serving idea Like many Asian noodle soups, this laksa is best served with both a spoon and chopsticks.

This popular spicy noodle soup originates in Malaysia and Singapore and is a favourite all over the world.

prawn laksa

1 tablespoon vegetable oil
2 x 400ml cans coconut milk
1 litre (4 cups) chicken stock
1 tablespoon brown sugar
2 teaspoons fish sauce
6 fresh kaffir lime leaves, shredded finely
1kg uncooked medium king prawns
250g fresh thin egg noodles
125g dried thin rice noodles
1 cup (80g) bean sprouts
¼ cup loosely packed fresh coriander leaves
1 lime, quartered

laksa paste

1 medium brown onion (150g), chopped coarsely
⅓ cup (80ml) coconut milk
2 tablespoons lime juice
1 tablespoon shrimp paste
2cm piece fresh ginger (10g), grated
1 tablespoon macadamias (10g), halved
10cm stick fresh lemon grass (20g), chopped finely
4 cloves garlic, quartered
2 fresh small red thai chillies, chopped coarsely
2 teaspoons ground coriander
2 teaspoons ground cumin
1 teaspoon ground turmeric

1 Make laksa paste.

2 Heat oil in large saucepan; cook laksa paste, stirring, about 5 minutes or until fragrant. Add coconut milk, stock, sugar, sauce and lime leaves; bring to the boil. Reduce heat; simmer, covered, 30 minutes.

3 Meanwhile, shell and devein prawns, leaving tails intact.

4 Place egg noodles in medium heatproof bowl, cover with boiling water; separate with fork, drain. Place rice noodles in same bowl, cover with boiling water; stand until just tender, drain.

5 Add prawns to laksa; cook, uncovered, until just changed in colour.

6 Divide noodles among serving bowls; ladle hot laksa into bowls. Top with sprouts and coriander; serve with lime.

laksa paste Blend or process ingredients until mixture forms a smooth paste.

prep & cook time 1 hour 15 minutes **serves** 4
nutritional count per serving 55.2g total fat (41.6g saturated fat); 3775kJ (903 cal); 56.6g carbohydrate; 42g protein; 7.6g fibre

sesame chicken stir-fry

350g bean thread vermicelli noodles
1 tablespoon peanut oil
2 chicken breast fillets (400g), sliced thinly
1 medium brown onion (150g), sliced thinly
1 clove garlic, crushed
300g broccolini, chopped coarsely
2 tablespoons fish sauce
1 tablespoon hot chilli sauce
2 tablespoons dark soy sauce
1 tablespoon toasted sesame seeds
1 fresh long red chilli, chopped finely
4 green onions, sliced thinly
1 cup (80g) bean sprouts

1 Place vermicelli in medium heatproof bowl, cover with boiling water; stand until just tender, drain.
2 Meanwhile, heat half the oil in wok; stir-fry chicken, in batches, until browned.
3 Heat remaining oil in wok; stir-fry brown onion, garlic and broccolini until onion softens.
4 Return chicken to wok with vermicelli, combined sauces, sesame seeds and half the chilli, half the green onion and half the sprouts; stir-fry just until hot.
5 Serve stir-fry topped with remaining chilli, green onion and sprouts.

prep & cook time 40 minutes **serves** 4
nutritional count per serving 9.3g total fat (1.6g saturated fat); 1325kJ (317 cal); 23.9g carbohydrate; 31.3g protein; 5.6g fibre.

hokkien mee

300g hokkien noodles
1 tablespoon peanut oil
700g beef rump steak, sliced thinly
1 medium brown onion (150g), sliced thinly
3cm piece fresh ginger (15g), grated
2 cloves garlic, crushed
2 fresh small red thai chillies, sliced thinly
1 small red capsicum (150g), sliced thinly
1 small green capsicum (150g), sliced thinly
200g mushrooms, quartered
2 tablespoons hoisin sauce
1 tablespoon dark soy sauce

1 Place noodles in medium heatproof bowl, cover with boiling water; separate with fork, drain.
2 Heat half the oil in wok; stir-fry beef, in batches, until browned.
3 Heat remaining oil in wok; stir-fry onion until soft. Add ginger, garlic and chilli; stir-fry until fragrant. Add capsicums and mushrooms; stir-fry until tender.
4 Return beef to wok with noodles and sauces; stir-fry until hot.

prep & cook time 30 minutes **serves** 4
nutritional count per serving 17.4g total fat (6.2g saturated fat); 1927kJ (461 cal); 27.2g carbohydrate; 46.1g protein; 5.3g fibre

sesame chicken stir-fry

hokkien mee

Nasi goreng literally means 'fried rice', but it's no ordinary fried rice — the addition of egg and prawns, as well as many spices and garnishes, make it something quite special.

nasi goreng

720g cooked medium king prawns
1 tablespoon peanut oil
175g dried chinese sausages, sliced thickly
1 medium brown onion (150g), sliced thinly
1 medium red capsicum (200g), sliced thinly
2 fresh long red chillies, sliced thinly
2 cloves garlic, crushed
2cm piece fresh ginger (10g), grated
1 teaspoon shrimp paste
4 cups (600g) cold cooked white long-grain rice
2 tablespoons kecap manis
1 tablespoon light soy sauce
4 green onions, sliced thinly
1 tablespoon peanut oil, extra
4 eggs

1 Shell and devein prawns.
2 Heat half the oil in wok; stir-fry sausage, in batches, until browned.
3 Heat remaining oil in wok; stir-fry onion, capsicum, chilli, garlic, ginger and paste, until vegetables soften. Add prawns and rice; stir-fry 2 minutes. Return sausage to wok with sauces and half the green onion; stir-fry until combined.
4 Heat extra oil in large frying pan; fry eggs, one side only, until just set. Divide nasi goreng among serving plates, top each with an egg; sprinkle with remaining green onion.

prep & cook time 40 minutes **serves** 4
nutritional count per serving 25.7g total fat (7.4g saturated fat); 2730kJ (653 cal); 48.5g carbohydrate; 54.7g protein; 3.3g fibre

The green colour in the curry paste comes from fresh green chillies, coriander and thai basil.

chicken green curry

1 tablespoon peanut oil
¼ cup (75g) green curry paste
3 long green chillies, chopped finely
1kg chicken thigh fillets, cut into 3cm pieces
2 x 400ml cans coconut milk
2 tablespoons fish sauce
2 tablespoons lime juice
1 tablespoon grated palm sugar
150g pea eggplants
1 large zucchini (150g), sliced thinly
⅓ cup loosely packed fresh thai basil leaves
¼ cup loosely packed fresh coriander leaves
2 green onions, chopped coarsely

1 Heat oil in large saucepan; cook paste and about two-thirds of the chilli, stirring, about 2 minutes or until fragrant. Add chicken; cook, stirring, until browned.
2 Add coconut milk, sauce, juice, sugar and eggplants; simmer, uncovered, about 10 minutes or until eggplants are just tender.
3 Add zucchini, basil and coriander; simmer, uncovered, until zucchini is just tender.
4 Serve curry sprinkled with remaining chilli and green onion.

prep & cook time 35 minutes **serves** 4
nutritional count per serving 67.3g total fat (43.2g saturated fat); 3716kJ (889 cal); 17g carbohydrate; 52.9g protein; 6g fibre

vietnamese prawn rolls

combination fried rice

vietnamese prawn rolls

50g rice vermicelli, soaked, drained
¼ small wombok (175g), shredded finely
½ cup loosely packed fresh mint leaves, torn
2 teaspoons brown sugar
2 tablespoons lime juice
500g cooked medium king prawns
12 x 21cm rice paper rounds
hoisin dipping sauce
½ cup (125ml) hoisin sauce
2 tablespoons rice vinegar

1 Combine chopped vermicelli in medium bowl with wombok, mint, sugar and juice.
2 Shell and devein prawns; chop meat finely.
3 Meanwhile, make hoisin dipping sauce.
4 Dip 1 rice paper round into bowl of warm water until soft; place on board covered with tea towel. Top with a little of the prawn meat and noodle filling. Fold and roll to enclose filling. Repeat with remaining rounds, prawn meat and noodle filling.
5 Serve with hoisin dipping sauce.
hoisin dipping sauce Combine ingredients in bowl.

prep & cook time 20 minutes **makes** 12
nutritional count per roll 0.9g total fat (0.1g saturated fat); 326kJ (78 cal); 10.8g carbohydrate; 5.5g protein; 1.7g fibre

combination fried rice

300g uncooked small king prawns
¼ cup (60ml) peanut oil
400g chicken breast fillets, sliced thinly
3 eggs, beaten lightly
4 rindless bacon rashers (260g), chopped coarsely
1 medium brown onion (150g), chopped finely
1 medium red capsicum (200g), chopped finely
2 cloves garlic, crushed
3cm piece fresh ginger (15g), grated
3 cups cooked white long-grain rice
2 tablespoons light soy sauce
¾ cup (90g) frozen peas
3 green onions, sliced thinly

1 Shell and devein prawns, leaving tails intact.
2 Heat 1 tablespoon of the oil in wok; stir-fry chicken, in batches, until cooked. Stir-fry prawns, in batches, until changed in colour.
3 Heat half the remaining oil in wok; stir-fry egg until just set then remove from wok.
4 Heat remaining oil in wok; stir-fry bacon, brown onion, capsicum, garlic and ginger until bacon is crisp. Return chicken, prawns and egg to wok with remaining ingredients; stir-fry until hot.

prep & cook time 40 minutes **serves** 4
nutritional count per serving 35.1g total fat (9.4g saturated fat); 3001kJ (718 cal); 46.5g carbohydrate; 52.3g protein; 3.9g fibre

Pad thai is a contrast of salty, sweet, sour and spicy flavours. Its garnish of roasted peanuts, crisp beansprouts and fried shallots add a crunch to the soft noodles, and the coriander and lime gives it a bit more bite.

pad thai

540g uncooked medium king prawns
¼ cup (85g) tamarind concentrate
⅓ cup (80ml) sweet chilli sauce
2 tablespoons fish sauce
⅓ cup firmly packed fresh coriander leaves
¼ cup (35g) roasted unsalted peanuts
¼ cup (20g) fried shallots
2 cups (160g) bean sprouts
4 green onions, sliced thinly
375g dried rice stick noodles
1 tablespoon peanut oil
2 cloves garlic, crushed
4cm piece fresh ginger (20g), grated
3 fresh small red thai chillies, chopped finely
250g pork mince
2 eggs, beaten lightly
1 lime, quartered

1 Shell and devein prawns, leaving tails intact.
2 Combine tamarind and sauces in small jug.
3 Combine coriander, nuts, shallots, half the sprouts and half the onion in medium bowl.
4 Place noodles in large heatproof bowl, cover with boiling water; stand until just tender, drain.
5 Meanwhile, heat oil in wok; stir-fry garlic, ginger and chilli until fragrant. Add pork; stir-fry until cooked. Add prawns; stir-fry 1 minute. Add egg; stir-fry until set. Add tamarind mixture, remaining sprouts and onion, and noodles; stir-fry until combined.
6 Divide mixture among serving bowls; sprinkle with coriander mixture, serve with lime wedges.

prep & cook time 35 minutes **serves** 4
nutritional count per serving 17.5g total fat (3.9g saturated fat); 1827kJ (437 cal); 30.3g carbohydrate; 36.8g protein; 4.9g fibre

thai beef salad

seafood and vegetable tempura

thai beef salad

800g piece beef rump steak

1 teaspoon peanut oil

250g bean thread vermicelli

1 telegraph cucumber (400g), halved lengthways, sliced thinly

1 large red capsicum (350g), sliced thinly

1 small red onion (100g), sliced thinly

1 fresh long red chilli, sliced thinly

1 cup firmly packed fresh mint leaves

1 cup firmly packed fresh coriander leaves

lime dressing

1 tablespoon coarsely chopped fresh coriander root and stem mixture

5 cloves garlic, chopped coarsely

1 teaspoon black peppercorns

½ cup (125ml) lime juice

1 tablespoon fish sauce

1 tablespoon grated palm sugar

2 x 10cm sticks fresh lemon grass (40g), chopped coarsely

1 Brush beef, both sides, with oil; cook on heated grill plate (or grill or barbecue) until cooked as desired. Cover beef; stand 5 minutes.

2 Place vermicelli in large heatproof bowl, cover with boiling water; stand until tender, drain. Cut vermicelli into random lengths into same bowl.

3 Meanwhile, make lime dressing.

4 Slice beef thinly; combine in large bowl with half the dressing and remaining ingredients. Drizzle remaining dressing over vermicelli. Divide vermicelli among shallow serving bowls; top with salad.

lime dressing Blend ingredients until chopped finely.

prep & cook time 30 minutes **serves** 6

nutritional count per serving 10.6g total fat (4.2g saturated fat); 1597kJ (382 cal); 34g carbohydrate; 35.3g protein; 3.4g fibre

seafood and vegetable tempura

540g uncooked medium king prawns

1 medium brown onion (150g)

peanut oil, for deep-frying

450g ocean trout fillets, cut into 3cm pieces

1 large red capsicum (350g), cut into 3cm pieces

1 small kumara (250g), sliced thinly

8 baby zucchini with flowers attached (160g), stamens removed

1 cup (150g) plain flour

1 lemon, cut into wedges

tempura batter

1 egg white

2 cups (500ml) cold soda water

1¼ cups (185g) plain flour

1¼ cups (185g) cornflour

lemon dipping sauce

½ cup (125ml) rice vinegar

¼ cup (55g) caster sugar

1 teaspoon light soy sauce

¼ teaspoon finely grated lemon rind

1 green onion (green part only), sliced thinly

1 Shell and devein prawns, leaving tails intact. Make three small cuts on the underside of each prawn, halfway through flesh, to prevent curling when cooked.

2 Halve onion from root end. Push 4 toothpicks, at regular intervals, through each onion half to hold rings together; cut in between toothpicks.

3 Make tempura batter. Make lemon dipping sauce.

4 Heat oil in wok. Dust prawns, onion, fish, capsicum, kumara and zucchini in flour; shake off excess. Dip, piece by piece, in batter; deep-fry until crisp. Drain on absorbent paper. Serve tempura with dipping sauce.

tempura batter Whisk egg white in large bowl until soft peaks form; add soda water, whisk to combine. Add sifted flours, whisk to combine (should be lumpy).

lemon dipping sauce Heat vinegar, sugar and sauce in small saucepan, stirring, until sugar dissolves. Remove from heat, add rind; stand 10 minutes. Strain sauce into serving dish; discard rind. Sprinkle with onion.

prep & cook time 1 hour **serves** 6

nutritional count per serving 16.6g total fat (3.1g saturated fat); 1831kJ (438 cal); 40.2g carbohydrate; 16.6g protein; 3.5g fibre

An Indian biryani differs from most rice dishes in that the rice and other ingredients are cooked separately. They're then layered, alternately and topped with fruit and nuts.

lamb biryani

1kg lamb shoulder, cut into 3cm pieces
3cm piece fresh ginger (15g), grated
2 cloves garlic, crushed
2 fresh small red thai chillies, chopped finely
2 teaspoons garam masala
1 tablespoon finely chopped fresh coriander
¼ teaspoon ground turmeric
½ cup (140g) yogurt
2 tablespoons ghee
½ cup (40g) flaked almonds
¼ cup (40g) sultanas
2 medium brown onions (300g), sliced thickly
½ cup (125ml) water
pinch saffron threads
1 tablespoon hot milk
1½ cups (300g) basmati rice
¼ cup firmly packed fresh coriander leaves

1 Combine lamb, ginger, garlic, chilli, garam masala, chopped coriander, turmeric and yogurt in medium bowl, cover; refrigerate overnight.
2 Heat half the ghee in large saucepan; cook nuts and sultanas, stirring, until nuts brown lightly. Remove from pan.
3 Heat remaining ghee in same pan; cook onion, covered, 5 minutes. Uncover; cook, stirring occasionally, about 5 minutes or until browned lightly. Reserve half of the onion.

4 Add lamb mixture to pan; cook, stirring, until browned. Add the water; bring to the boil. Reduce heat; simmer, covered, 1 hour. Uncover; simmer about 30 minutes or until lamb is tender and sauce is thickened.
5 Meanwhile, combine saffron and milk in small bowl; stand 15 minutes.
6 Cook rice in medium saucepan of boiling water, uncovered, 5 minutes; drain.
7 Preheat oven to 180°C/160°C fan-forced.
8 Spread half the lamb mixture into oiled deep 2-litre (8-cup) ovenproof dish. Layer with half the rice; top with remaining lamb mixture then remaining rice. Drizzle milk mixture over rice; cover tightly with greased foil and lid. Bake about 30 minutes or until rice is tender.
9 Serve biryani topped with reserved onion, nut and sultana mixture and coriander leaves.

prep & cook time 2 hours 35 minutes (+ refrigeration)
serves 4
nutritional count per serving 38.6g total fat (17.4g saturated fat); 3703kJ (886 cal); 73.8g carbohydrate; 58.7g protein; 3.4g fibre

caesar salad

1 small french bread stick (150g)

¼ cup (60ml) olive oil

1 clove garlic, crushed

4 rindless bacon rashers (260g)

1 large cos lettuce, trimmed, chopped coarsely

3 green onions, sliced thinly

1 cup (80g) flaked parmesan cheese

4 hard-boiled eggs, quartered

caesar dressing

2 egg yolks

1 clove garlic, quartered

1 anchovy fillet

1 tablespoon lemon juice

1 tablespoon worcestershire sauce

2 teaspoons dijon mustard

½ cup (125ml) olive oil

1 Preheat oven to 180°C/160°C fan-forced.

2 Make caesar dressing.

3 Halve bread lengthways; slice halves thinly. Combine oil and garlic in large bowl with bread; place bread on oven tray. Toast bread in oven until croûtons are brown.

4 Meanwhile, cook bacon in heated large frying pan until crisp; drain on absorbent paper. Chop coarsely.

5 Combine lettuce, half the croûtons, half the bacon, half the onion, half the cheese and half the dressing in large bowl.

6 Divide salad among serving bowls; top with egg and remaining ingredients. Drizzle with remaining dressing.

caesar dressing Blend or process egg yolks, garlic, anchovy, juice, sauce and mustard until smooth. With motor operating, gradually add oil in a thin, steady stream; process until mixture thickens. Stir in about a tablespoon of warm water to make dressing pourable.

prep & cook time 30 minutes **serves** 4
nutritional count per serving 62.4g total fat (14g saturated fat); 3394kJ (812 cal); 25.4g carbohydrate; 36.2g protein; 5.7g fibre

waldorf salad

¾ cup (225g) mayonnaise
¼ cup (60ml) lemon juice
5 stalks celery (750g), trimmed, sliced thickly
2 medium red apples (300g), sliced thinly
1 small red onion (100g), sliced thinly
1 cup (100g) roasted walnuts
1 cup loosely packed fresh flat-leaf parsley leaves

1 Combine mayonnaise and juice in large bowl; mix in remaining ingredients.

prep time 20 minutes **serves** 4
nutritional count per serving 35.7g total fat (3.1g saturated fat); 1852kJ (443 cal); 22.4g carbohydrate; 5.8g protein; 6.3g fibre

note This classic dish literally means 'chilli with meat'. Feel free to pep it up with more chilli or tone it down by reducing the cayenne and jalapeño chillies. It is also excellent served on a jacket potato, on couscous or with

chilli con carne

1 cup (200g) dried kidney beans
1.5kg beef chuck steak
2 litres (8 cups) water
1 tablespoon olive oil
2 medium brown onions (300g), chopped coarsely
2 cloves garlic, crushed
2 teaspoons ground cumin
2 teaspoons ground coriander
½ teaspoon cayenne pepper
2 teaspoons sweet paprika
2 x 400g cans crushed tomatoes
1 tablespoon tomato paste
4 green onions, chopped coarsely
2 tablespoons coarsely chopped fresh coriander
⅓ cup (65g) finely chopped bottled jalapeño chillies

1 Place beans in medium bowl; cover with water; stand overnight, drain.
2 Combine beef with the water in large saucepan; bring to the boil. Reduce heat, simmer, covered, 1½ hours.
3 Drain beef in large muslin-lined strainer over bowl; reserve 3½ cups (875ml) of the cooking liquid. Using two forks, shred beef.
4 Heat oil in same pan; cook brown onion and garlic, stirring, until onion is soft. Add spices; cook, stirring, until fragrant. Add beans, undrained tomatoes, paste and 2 cups of the reserved liquid; bring to the boil. Reduce heat, simmer, covered, 1 hour.
5 Add beef and remaining reserved liquid to pan; simmer, covered, about 30 minutes or until beans are tender. Remove from heat; stir in green onions, coriander and chilli. Serve chilli con carne with steamed rice, if you like.

prep & cook time 3 hours 45 minutes (+ standing)
serves 8
nutritional count per serving 11.4g total fat (3.9g saturated fat); 1496kJ (358 cal); 14.7g carbohydrate; 45.1g protein; 7.6g fibre

tip Mexe-beans are kidney beans
with some spices already added.
Look for them in the international
section of your supermarket with
other Mexican-style ingredients, or
try refried beans instead.

How fiery a chilli is can be judged by how
wide the 'shoulders' on it are.
The wider the area that joins the chilli
to the stem, the milder it is.

bean and coriander quesadillas

2 x 425g cans mexe-beans, drained, mashed
8 large (20cm) flour tortillas (300g)
2 large tomatoes (440g), seeded, chopped finely
2 fresh long red chillies, chopped finely
½ cup finely chopped fresh coriander
1¼ cups (150g) coarsely grated cheddar cheese

1 Preheat sandwich press.
2 Spread beans over four tortillas. Sprinkle with tomato, chilli, coriander and cheese. Top with remaining tortillas.
3 Cook quesadillas in sandwich press until browned both sides and heated through; cut into wedges. Serve accompanied with sour cream, if you like.

prep & cook time 15 minutes **serves** 4
nutritional count per serving 15g total fat (8.4g saturated fat); 1898kJ (454 cal); 49.5g carbohydrate; 23.3g protein; 13.4g fibre

tabbouleh

¼ cup (40g) burghul
3 medium tomatoes (450g)
3 cups coarsely chopped fresh flat-leaf parsley
3 green onions, chopped finely
½ cup coarsely chopped fresh mint
1 clove garlic, crushed
¼ cup (60ml) lemon juice
¼ cup (60ml) olive oil

1 Place burghul in shallow medium bowl. Halve tomatoes, scoop pulp from tomato over burghul. Chop tomato flesh finely; spread over burghul. Cover; refrigerate 1 hour.
2 Combine burghul mixture in large bowl with remaining ingredients.

prep time 30 minutes (+ refrigeration) **serves** 4
nutritional count per serving 14.2g total fat (2g saturated fat); 790kJ (189 cal); 9.4g carbohydrate; 3.6g protein; 5.9g fibre

greek salad with grilled lamb

¼ cup (70g) yogurt
⅓ cup (80ml) lemon juice
¼ cup (60ml) olive oil
2 cloves garlic, crushed
600g lamb fillets
3 medium tomatoes (450g), cut into thin wedges
1 small red onion (100g), sliced thinly
2 medium red capsicums (400g), chopped coarsely
2 lebanese cucumbers (260g), chopped coarsely
½ cup (75g) seeded kalamata olives
400g can chickpeas, rinsed, drained
1 cup firmly packed fresh flat-leaf parsley leaves
100g fetta cheese, crumbled

1 Combine yogurt, 1 tablespoon of the juice, 1 tablespoon of the oil and half the garlic in medium bowl, add lamb; mix well. Cover; refrigerate until needed.
2 Meanwhile, place remaining juice, oil and garlic in screw-top jar; shake well.
3 Drain lamb; discard marinade. Cook lamb on heated oiled grill plate (or grill or barbecue) until cooked as desired. Cover; stand 5 minutes then slice thickly.
4 Combine remaining ingredients in large bowl with lemon dressing. Serve salad topped with lamb.

prep & cook time 25 minutes (+ refrigeration)
serves 6
nutritional count per serving 27.5g total fat (8.8g saturated fat); 2215kJ (530 cal); 23.1g carbohydrate; 44g protein; 7.8g fibre

coq au vin

800g spring onions
¼ cup (60ml) olive oil
6 rindless bacon rashers (390g), chopped coarsely
300g button mushrooms
2 cloves garlic, crushed
8 chicken thigh fillets (880g)
¼ cup (35g) plain flour
2 cups (500ml) dry red wine
1½ cups (375ml) chicken stock
2 tablespoons tomato paste
3 bay leaves
4 sprigs fresh thyme
2 sprigs fresh rosemary

1 Trim green ends from onions, leaving about 4cm of stem attached; trim roots. Heat 1 tablespoon of the oil in large frying pan; cook onions, stirring, until browned all over; remove from pan.
2 Add bacon, mushrooms and garlic to pan; cook, stirring, until bacon is crisp, remove from pan.
3 Coat chicken in flour; shake off excess. Heat remaining oil in same pan. Cook chicken, in batches, until browned all over; drain on absorbent paper.
4 Return chicken to pan with wine, stock, paste, bay leaves, herbs, onions and bacon mixture. Bring to the boil; reduce heat, simmer, uncovered, about 35 minutes or until chicken is tender and sauce has thickened slightly.

prep & cook time 1 hour 30 minutes **serves** 4
nutritional count per serving 43.6g total fat (11.8g saturated fat); 3428kJ (820 cal); 16.3g carbohydrate; 67.8g protein; 6.4g fibre

boeuf bourguignon

300g baby brown onions
2 tablespoons olive oil
2kg gravy beef, trimmed, chopped coarsely
30g butter
4 rindless bacon rashers (260g), chopped coarsely
400g button mushrooms, halved
2 cloves garlic, crushed
¼ cup (35g) plain flour
1¼ cups (310ml) beef stock
2½ cups (625ml) dry red wine
2 bay leaves
2 sprigs fresh thyme
½ cup coarsely chopped fresh flat-leaf parsley

1 Peel onions, leaving root end intact so onion remains whole during cooking.
2 Heat oil in large flameproof dish; cook beef, in batches, until browned.
3 Add butter to dish; cook onions, bacon, mushrooms and garlic, stirring, until onions are browned lightly.
4 Sprinkle flour over onion mixture; cook, stirring, until flour mixture thickens and bubbles. Gradually add stock and wine; stir over heat until mixture boils and thickens. Return beef and any juices to dish, add bay leaves and thyme; bring to the boil. Reduce heat; simmer, covered, about 2 hours or until beef is tender, stirring every 30 minutes.
5 Remove pan from heat; discard bay leaves. Stir in parsley.

prep & cook time 2 hours 45 minutes **serves** 6
nutritional count per serving 31.4g total fat (12.1g saturated fat); 2658kJ (636 cal); 6.6g carbohydrate; 80.3g protein; 2.8g fibre

pecan pie

1 cup (120g) pecans, chopped coarsely
2 tablespoons cornflour
1 cup (220g) firmly packed brown sugar
60g butter, melted
2 tablespoons cream
1 teaspoon vanilla extract
3 eggs
⅓ cup (40g) pecans, extra
2 tablespoons apricot jam, warmed, sieved

pastry
1¼ cups (185g) plain flour
⅓ cup (55g) icing sugar
125g cold butter, chopped
1 egg yolk
1 teaspoon water

1 Make pastry.

2 Grease 24cm-round loose-based flan tin. Roll pastry between sheets of baking paper until large enough to line tin. Ease pastry into tin, press into base and side; trim edge. Cover; refrigerate 30 minutes.

3 Preheat oven to 180°C/160°C fan-forced.

4 Place tin on oven tray. Line pastry case with baking paper, fill with dried beans or rice. Bake 10 minutes; remove paper and beans carefully from pie shell. Bake about 5 minutes; cool.

5 Reduce oven temperature to 160°C/140°C fan-forced.

6 Combine chopped nuts and cornflour in medium bowl. Add sugar, butter, cream, extract and eggs; stir until combined. Pour mixture into shell, sprinkle with extra nuts.

7 Bake pie about 45 minutes. Cool; brush with jam.

pastry Process flour, icing sugar and butter until crumbly. Add egg yolk and the water; process until ingredients just come together. Knead dough on floured surface until smooth. Cover; refrigerate 30 minutes.

prep & cook time 1 hour 25 minutes (+ refrigeration)
serves 10
nutritional count per serving 30.8g total fat (12.5g saturated fat); 2023kJ (484 cal); 46.5g carbohydrate; 6.3g protein; 2.1g fibre

This sticky sweet-textured pie is a
specialty of America's South.

This upside-down tart is a French classic. The traditional recipe uses apples but you could easily replace them with pears or even bananas.

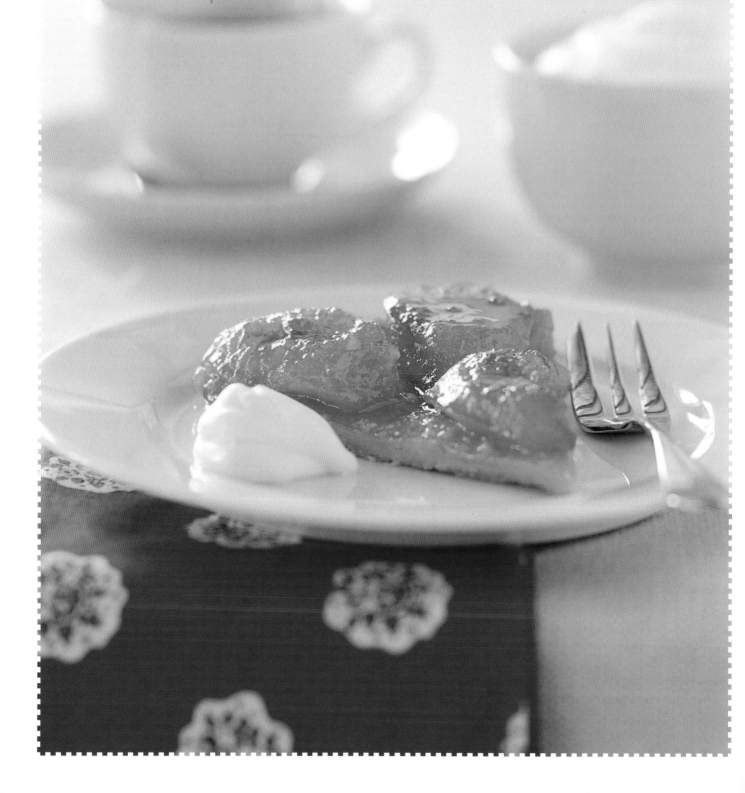

tarte tatin

2 tablespoons orange juice
⅔ cup (150g) caster sugar
70g butter
3 medium apples (450g), peeled
pastry
1 cup (150g) plain flour
80g cold butter, chopped
1 tablespoon caster sugar
1 tablespoon cold water, approximately

1 Combine juice, sugar and butter in 23cm heavy-based ovenproof frying pan; stir over heat, without boiling, until sugar is dissolved. Simmer, stirring occasionally, until mixture becomes a thick, light golden caramel. Remove from heat.

2 Halve apples; cut each half into 3 wedges, remove cores. Pack apple wedges tightly into pan over caramel, return to heat; simmer, uncovered, about 15 minutes or until most of the liquid is evaporated and caramel is dark golden brown. Remove from heat; cool 1 hour.

3 Preheat oven to 180°C/160°C fan-forced.

4 Roll pastry into circle a little larger than the pan. Lift pastry, without stretching it, on top of apples, tuck inside edge of pan. Bake in oven about 25 minutes or until pastry is golden brown and crisp. Remove tart from oven, stand 5 minutes. Carefully invert tart onto plate. Serve warm with cream, if desired.

pastry Blend or process flour, butter and sugar until mixture resembles fine breadcrumbs. Add just enough water to make ingredients just cling together. Knead dough on floured surface until smooth. Cover; refrigerate 1 hour.

prep & cook time 1 hour 15 minutes (+ refrigeration & cooling) **serves** 6
nutritional count per serving 20.9g total fat (13.6g saturated fat); 1705kJ (408 cal); 53.1g carbohydrate; 3.1g protein; 2g fibre

panna cotta with fresh figs

new york cheesecake

Bring a rainbow of colour to the kitchen
and inspire your budding young chefs.

The kids will love creating their own Mexican fiesta with these taco treats.

beef tacos

2 teaspoons olive oil
500g beef mince
1 clove garlic, crushed
1½ cups (375ml) water
2 tablespoons tomato paste
35g packet taco seasoning
12 taco shells
8 lettuce leaves, shredded finely
2 medium tomatoes (300g), chopped finely
1 cup (120g) grated cheddar cheese
½ cup bottled mild chunky salsa

1 Preheat oven to 180°C/160°C fan-forced.
2 Heat oil in large frying pan; cook beef and garlic, stirring, about 5 minutes or until beef is browned all over. Add the water, paste and taco seasoning; stir until well combined, bring to the boil. Reduce heat; simmer, uncovered, about 10 minutes or until most of the liquid is evaporated.
3 Meanwhile, place taco shells, upside down, on oven tray. Heat shells in oven, uncovered, about 5 minutes or until heated through. Using oven mitts, remove tray from oven, place on a wooden board.
4 Divide beef mixture among taco shells; top with lettuce, tomato and cheese, drizzle with salsa

prep & cook time 40 minutes **makes** 12
nutritional count per taco 10.9g total fat (3.9g saturated fat); 874kJ (209 cal); 12.7g carbohydrate; 13.6g protein; 2.9g fibre

meat pie scrolls

1 tablespoon olive oil
1 small brown onion (80g), chopped finely
1 clove garlic, crushed
3 rindless bacon rashers (195g), chopped finely
300g beef mince
400g can diced tomatoes
1 tablespoon tomato paste
2 tablespoons worcestershire sauce
½ cup (125ml) beef stock
¼ cup coarsely chopped fresh flat-leaf parsley
2 cups (300g) self-raising flour
1 tablespoon caster sugar
50g butter, chopped coarsely
¾ cup (180ml) milk
1 cup (110g) pizza cheese

1 Heat oil in large frying pan; cook onion, garlic and bacon, stirring, until onion softens. Add beef; cook, stirring, until beef changes colour. Add undrained tomatoes, paste, sauce and stock; bring to the boil. Reduce heat; simmer, uncovered, about 20 minutes or until sauce thickens. Remove from heat; stir in parsley. Cool.
2 Preheat oven to 180°C/160°C fan-forced. Grease two six-hole (¾-cup/180ml) texas muffin pans.
3 Sift flour and sugar into medium bowl; rub in butter with fingers. Stir in milk; mix to a soft, sticky dough. Knead dough on floured surface; roll dough out to 30cm x 40cm rectangle.
4 Spread beef mixture over dough; sprinkle with cheese. Roll dough tightly from one long side; trim ends. Cut roll into 12 slices; place one slice in each pan hole.
5 Bake scrolls about 25 minutes. Serve top-side up.

prep & cook time 1 hour 15 minutes **makes** 12
nutritional count per scroll 11g total fat (5.4g saturated fat); 1024kJ (245 cal); 22.3g carbohydrate; 13.3g protein; 1.6g fibre

chicken sausage rolls

1kg chicken mince
1 medium brown onion (150g), chopped finely
½ cup (35g) stale breadcrumbs
1 egg
¼ cup finely chopped fresh basil
½ cup (75g) drained semi-dried tomatoes in oil, chopped finely
2 tablespoons tomato paste
5 sheets puff pastry
1 egg, extra

1 Preheat oven to 220°C/200°C fan-forced. Line oven trays with baking paper.
2 Combine mince, onion, breadcrumbs, egg, basil, semi-dried tomato and paste in large bowl.
3 Cut pastry sheets in half lengthways. Place equal amounts of chicken filling mixture lengthways along centre of each pastry piece; roll pastry to enclose filling. Cut each roll into six pieces; place, seam-side down, on trays. Brush with extra egg.
4 Bake rolls about 30 minutes. Serve hot, with tomato sauce.

prep & cook time 45 minutes **makes** 60
nutritional count per serving 4.8g total fat (2.2g saturated fat); 359kJ (86 cal); 6g carbohydrate; 4.5g protein; 0.5g fibre

meat pie scrolls

chicken sausage rolls

serving idea This is a clever way to make sure your kids get their vegies. You could also use other vegetables in here too – try grated carrot, zucchini or capsicum.

chocolate sundaes

2 litres vanilla ice-cream
½ cup (70g) crushed nuts
12 ice-cream wafers
100g marshmallows
hot chocolate sauce
200g dark eating chocolate, chopped coarsely
½ cup (125ml) thickened cream

1 Make hot chocolate sauce.
2 Place a little of the hot chocolate sauce in the bottom of six ¾-cup (180ml) serving glasses; top with ice-cream, more chocolate sauce, nuts, wafers and marshmallows.
hot chocolate sauce Stir chocolate and cream in small saucepan over low heat until chocolate is melted and sauce is smooth; do not overheat.

prep & cook time 10 minutes **serves** 6
nutritional count per serving 41.4g total fat (23.5g saturated fat); 2863kJ (685 cal); 72.1g carbohydrate; 11.8g protein; 1.4g fibre

tropical fruit skewers with orange glaze

strawberry jelly cakes

tropical fruit skewers with orange glaze

1 teaspoon finely grated orange rind
¼ cup (60ml) orange juice
2 tablespoons brown sugar
2 medium bananas (400g)
250g strawberries
600g piece pineapple
1 star fruit (160g)
200g low-fat vanilla yogurt

1 Stir rind, juice and sugar in small saucepan over low heat until sugar dissolves. Cool.
2 Preheat grill.
3 Peel bananas; slice thickly crossways. Hull and halve strawberries. Peel pineapple; cut into chunks. Slice star fruit thickly.
4 Thread fruits, alternately, onto skewers. Place skewers on oven tray lined with baking paper; pour orange mixture over skewers.
5 Grill skewers, turning occasionally, 10 minutes or until browned lightly. Serve with yogurt.

prep & cook time 35 minutes **serves** 4
nutritional count per serving 0.5g total fat (0.1g saturated fat); 974kJ (233 cal); 45.9g carbohydrate; 7.1g protein; 7.3g fibre

strawberry jelly cakes

125g butter, softened
½ teaspoon vanilla extract
½ cup (110g) caster sugar
2 eggs
1½ cups (225g) self-raising flour
⅓ cup (80ml) low-fat milk
1¾ cups (430ml) boiling water
85g packet strawberry jelly crystals
2 tablespoons passionfruit pulp
3 cups (225g) shredded coconut

1 Preheat oven to 180°C/160°C fan-forced. Grease deep 23cm-square cake pan; line base with baking paper.
2 Beat butter, extract and sugar in small bowl with electric mixer until light and fluffy. Add eggs, one at a time; beat until just combined. Stir in flour and milk until smooth; spread mixture into pan.
3 Bake about 25 minutes. Stand 5 minutes; turn, top-side up, onto wire rack to cool.
4 Meanwhile, stir the water and jelly in medium heatproof jug until crystals dissolve; stir pulp into jelly. Pour into 19cm x 29cm slice pan; refrigerate, stirring occasionally, until set to the consistency of unbeaten egg white.
5 Cut cake into 36 squares; dip each square into jelly then toss in coconut. Stand jelly cakes on tray; cover, refrigerate 30 minutes.

prep & cook time 1 hour 10 minutes (+ refrigeration)
makes 36
nutritional count per cake 6.7g total fat (5g saturated fat); 456kJ (109 cal); 10.2g carbohydrate; 1g protein; 1.2g fibre

serving idea Serve this deliciously gooey pudding with ice-cream, and drizzle the chocolate sauce over the ice-cream as well.

chocolate self-saucing pudding

60g butter
½ cup (125ml) milk
½ teaspoon vanilla extract
¾ cup (165g) caster sugar
1 cup (150g) self-raising flour
1 tablespoon cocoa powder
¾ cup (165g) firmly packed brown sugar
1 tablespoon cocoa powder, extra
2 cups (500ml) boiling water

1 Preheat oven to 180°C/160°C fan-forced. Grease 1.5-litre (6-cup) ovenproof dish.
2 Melt butter with milk in medium saucepan. Remove from heat; stir in extract and caster sugar then sifted flour and cocoa. Spread mixture into dish.
3 Sift brown sugar and extra cocoa over mixture; gently pour boiling water over mixture.
4 Bake pudding 40 minutes or until centre is firm. Stand 5 minutes before serving.

prep & cook time 1 hour **serves** 6
nutritional count per serving 9.7g total fat (6.2g saturated fat); 1618kJ (387 cal); 73.4g carbohydrate; 3.8g protein; 1.1g fibre

apple berry crumbles

2 medium apples (300g)
¾ cup (115g) frozen mixed berries
2 tablespoons lemon juice
2 tablespoons brown sugar
2 tablespoons plain flour
¼ cup (20g) rolled oats
20g butter
¼ cup (30g) finely chopped roasted hazelnuts

1 Preheat oven to 200°C/180°C fan-forced. Grease four ¾-cup (180ml) ovenproof dishes; place on oven tray.
2 Peel and core apples; chop coarsely. Combine apple, berries, juice and half the sugar in medium bowl; divide mixture among dishes.
3 Combine remaining sugar, flour and oats in small bowl. Rub butter into flour mixture; stir in nuts. Divide crumble over fruit mixture, pressing down firmly.
4 Bake crumbles 30 minutes or until browned lightly. Dust with sifted icing sugar and serve with yogurt.

prep & cook time 45 minutes **serves** 4
nutritional count per serving 9.3g total fat (3g saturated fat); 803kJ (192 cal); 22.3g carbohydrate; 3.1g protein; 3.1g fibre

after-school snacks

Being at school all day is tiring – your little learners will be ravenous.

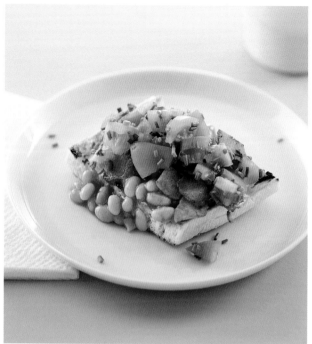

bruschetta fingers

1 small turkish bread roll (160g)
2 teaspoons sun-dried tomato pesto
6 cherry tomatoes, quartered
30g cherry bocconcini cheese, sliced thinly
1 tablespoon finely chopped fresh flat-leaf parsley

1 Split bread in half; toast, cut-side up, then cut into fingers.
2 Spread toasted sides with pesto; top with tomato and cheese then sprinkle with parsley.

prep & cook time 10 minutes **serves** 1
nutritional count per serving 14.5g total fat (4.7g saturated fat); 2358kJ (569 cal); 81.9g carbohydrate; 22.5g protein; 6.1g fibre

baked beans, bacon and tomato on toast

1 medium tomato (150g), chopped coarsely
2 teaspoons finely chopped chives
½ x 420g can baked beans in tomato sauce
2 rindless bacon rashers (1130g), chopped coarsely
¼ large loaf turkish bread (105g), halved

1 Preheat grill.
2 Combine tomato and chives in small bowl.
3 Heat beans in small saucepan.
4 Meanwhile, cook bacon in heated small frying pan, stirring, until crisp; drain on absorbent paper.
5 Cut bread pieces horizontally; toast cut sides.
Top toast with beans, bacon and tomato mixture; grill about 2 minutes or until hot.

prep & cook time 10 minutes **serves** 2
nutritional count per serving 10.4g total fat (3.2g saturated fat); 1450kJ (347 cal); 37.5g carbohydrate; 22g protein; 7.4g fibre

banana smoothie

1 cups (250ml) skim milk
1 medium banana (230g), chopped coarsely
2 tablespoons low-fat yogurt
1 teaspoon honey
1 teaspoon wheat germ
pinch ground cinnamon

1 Blend or process ingredients until smooth.

prep time 5 minutes **serves** 1
nutritional count per serving 0.4g total fat (0.2g
saturated fat); 648kJ (155 cal); 28.3g carbohydrate;
8.3g protein; 1.8g fibre

apple and pear juice

1 medium apple (150g)
1 medium pear (230g)

1 Cut apple and pear into wedges.
2 Push fruit through juice extractor into glass;
stir to combine.

prep & cook time 5 minutes **serves** 1
nutritional count per serving 0.4g total fat (0g
saturated fat); 853kJ (204 cal); 51.3g carbohydrate;
1.1g protein; 9g fibre

These healthy snacks are fun to eat. And kids always love to eat things where they can break the 'don't play with your food' rule.

noodle and vegetable rolls

60g rice vermicelli noodles
½ medium carrot (60g), grated coarsely
½ small wombok (350g), shredded finely
1 tablespoon fish sauce
1 tablespoon brown sugar
¼ cup (60ml) lemon juice
12 x 17cm-square rice paper sheets
12 large fresh mint leaves
sweet chilli dipping sauce
¼ cup (60ml) sweet chilli sauce
1 tablespoon fish sauce
1 tablespoon lime juice

1 Place noodles in medium heatproof bowl, cover with boiling water; stand until just tender, drain. Using kitchen scissors, cut noodles into random lengths.
2 Place noodles in medium bowl with carrot, wombok, sauce, sugar and juice; toss gently to combine.
3 To assemble rolls, place one sheet of rice paper in medium bowl of warm water until just softened; lift sheet carefully from water, placing it on a tea-towel-covered board with a corner point facing towards you. Place a little of the vegetable filling and one mint leaf vertically along centre of sheet; fold top and bottom corners over filling then roll sheet from side to side to enclose filling. Repeat with remaining rice paper sheets, vegetable filling and mint leaves.
4 Combine ingredients for sweet chilli dipping sauce in small bowl.
5 Serve rolls with dipping sauce.

prep & cook time 25 minutes **makes** 12 rolls
nutritional count per roll 0.2g total fat (0g saturated fat); 188kJ (45 cal); 9g carbohydrate; 1.4g protein; 0.8g fibre
nutritional count per tablespoon dipping sauce 0.4g total fat (0.1g saturated fat); 71kJ (17 cal); 2.7g carbohydrate; 0.4g protein; 0.6g fibre

tip If sweet chilli sauce is too spicy for your kids, try plum sauce instead.

tomato, spinach and cheese melts

barbecued chicken pizza

tomato, spinach and cheese melts

30g baby spinach leaves
1 medium tomatoes (150g), sliced thinly
⅔ cup (60g) grated cheddar cheese
4 english muffins or crumpets

1 Preheat grill.
2 Layer spinach leaves, tomato and cheese between muffins.
3 Place under grill 5 minutes or until cheese melts.

prep & cook time 15 minutes **makes** 2
nutritional count per serving 7.8g total fat (4.5g saturated fat); 949kJ (227 cal); 24.9g carbohydrate; 12.5g protein; 3.2g fibre

barbecued chicken pizza

1 sheet puff pastry
2 tablespoons barbecue sauce
½ cup (80g) shredded barbecued chicken
20g drained, coarsely chopped roasted red capsicum
½ green onion, sliced thinly
½ cup (50g) pizza cheese

1 Preheat oven to 200°C/180°C fan-forced. Oil oven tray.
2 Cut four 11.5cm rounds from pastry; place on tray.
3 Spread rounds with sauce; top with chicken, capsicum, onion and cheese.
4 Bake pizzas about 15 minutes or until browned.

prep & cook time 30 minutes **makes** 4
nutritional count per pizza 14.7g total fat (3.1g saturated fat); 1074kJ (257 cal); 20.3g carbohydrate; 10.7g protein; 0.8g fibre

This protein-rich snack will keep the kids
going until dinnertime — and buy
you some time to get dinner ready.

ham, egg and cheese toastie

2 slices wholemeal bread (90g)
1 tablespoon barbecue sauce
30g shaved ham
1 hard-boiled egg, sliced thinly
¼ cup (30g) coarsely grated reduced-fat
  cheddar cheese

1 Spread bread with sauce; sandwich ham, egg and cheese between bread slices.
2 Toast in sandwich press until golden brown.

prep & cook time 10 minutes **makes** 1
nutritional count per toastie 16.1g total fat (6.9g saturated fat); 1898kJ (454 cal); 44.3g carbohydrate; 29.7g protein; 5.9g fibre

frozen fruit yogurt blocks

rhubarb, muesli and yogurt cups

frozen fruit yogurt blocks

1½ cups (420g) vanilla yogurt
1 cup (150g) frozen mixed berries
1 tablespoon honey

1 Combine yogurt, berries and honey in medium bowl.
2 Spoon mixture into six ¼-cup (60ml) ice-block moulds. Press lids on firmly; freeze 6 hours or overnight.

prep time 5 minutes (+ freezing) **makes** 6
nutritional count per block 2.5g total fat (1.5g saturated fat); 389kJ (93 cal); 12.6g carbohydrate; 3.8g protein; 1.5g fibre

rhubarb, muesli and yogurt cups

2 cups (220g) coarsely chopped fresh
  rhubarb stalks
¼ cup (55g) caster sugar
½ cup (125ml) water
½ teaspoon ground cinnamon
1⅓ cups (375g) low-fat vanilla yogurt
⅓ cup (45g) toasted muesli

1 Place rhubarb, sugar, the water and cinnamon in medium saucepan; bring to the boil. Reduce heat; simmer, uncovered, stirring occasionally, 10 minutes or until rhubarb is tender. Transfer to medium heatproof bowl; cover, refrigerate 1 hour.
2 Divide rhubarb mixture among four ¾-cup (180ml) serving glasses; top with yogurt then muesli.

prep & cook time 20 minutes (+ refrigeration)
serves 4
nutritional count per serving 1.5g total fat (0.5g saturated fat); 782kJ (187 cal); 33.9g carbohydrate; 7.4g protein; 2.9g fibre

apple and raisin french toast

1 small apple (130g)
1 tablespoon water
2 tablespoons coarsely chopped raisins
¼ loaf unsliced white bread (160g)
2 eggs
¼ cup (60ml) low-fat milk
2 teaspoons honey
pinch ground cinnamon
10g butter
1 tablespoon icing sugar

1 Peel, core then thinly slice apple.
2 Place apple and the water in small saucepan; bring to the boil. Reduce heat; simmer, covered, about 5 minutes or until apple is just tender. Remove from heat; stir in raisins. Cool 15 minutes.
3 Meanwhile, slice bread into quarters; cut each piece three-quarters of the way through. Divide apple mixture among bread pockets.
4 Whisk eggs in medium bowl; whisk in milk, honey and cinnamon.
5 Heat half the butter in large frying pan. Dip two bread pockets into egg mixture, one at a time; cook, uncovered, until browned both sides.
6 Remove from pan; cover to keep warm. Repeat with remaining butter and bread. Cut pockets into quarters; serve sprinkled with sifted icing sugar.

prep & cook time 30 minutes (+ cooling) **serves** 2
nutritional count per serving 10.3g total fat (4.3g saturated fat); 1668kJ (399 cal); 60.6g carbohydrate; 13.6g protein; 3.5g fibre

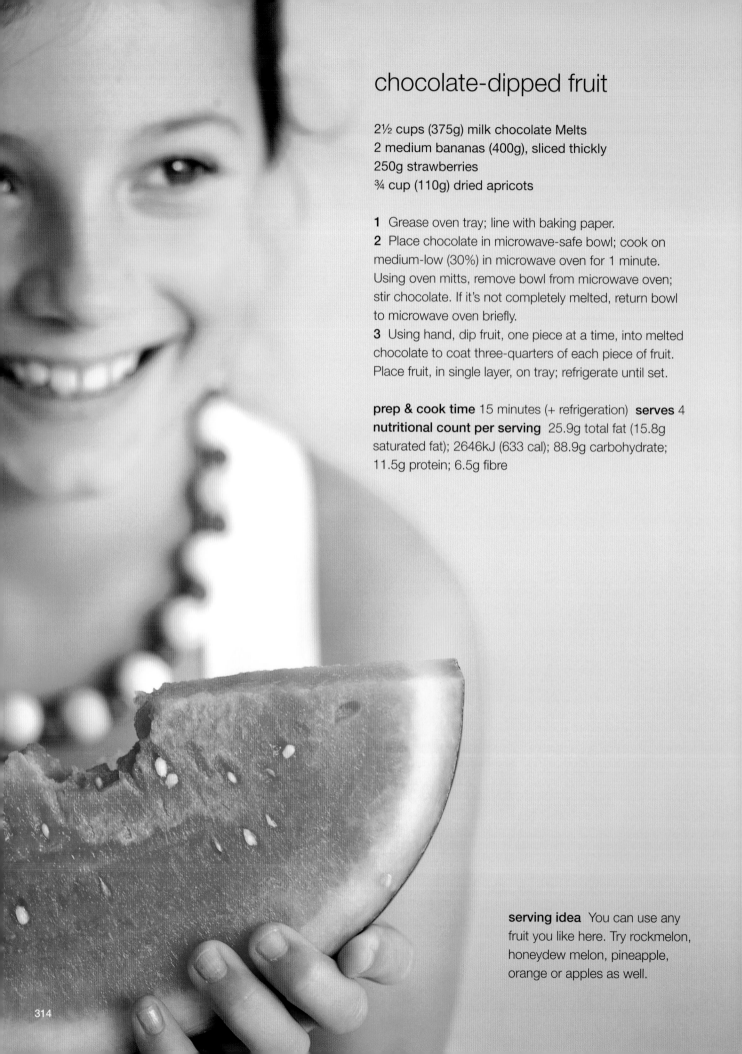

chocolate-dipped fruit

2½ cups (375g) milk chocolate Melts
2 medium bananas (400g), sliced thickly
250g strawberries
¾ cup (110g) dried apricots

1 Grease oven tray; line with baking paper.
2 Place chocolate in microwave-safe bowl; cook on medium-low (30%) in microwave oven for 1 minute. Using oven mitts, remove bowl from microwave oven; stir chocolate. If it's not completely melted, return bowl to microwave oven briefly.
3 Using hand, dip fruit, one piece at a time, into melted chocolate to coat three-quarters of each piece of fruit. Place fruit, in single layer, on tray; refrigerate until set.

prep & cook time 15 minutes (+ refrigeration) **serves** 4
nutritional count per serving 25.9g total fat (15.8g saturated fat); 2646kJ (633 cal); 88.9g carbohydrate; 11.5g protein; 6.5g fibre

serving idea You can use any fruit you like here. Try rockmelon, honeydew melon, pineapple, orange or apples as well.

314

These delicious fruity snacks also make
a great dessert for both kids and adults.
Make an extra batch at the same time and
refrigerate them until dessert time.

pears on fruit toast

lemonade ice-blocks

pears on fruit toast

2 slices fruit bread
½ small pear (180g), sliced thinly
1 teaspoon brown sugar

1 Preheat grill.
2 Toast fruit bread.
3 Place pear slices on each slice of toast.
4 Sprinkle pear with sugar. Toast under grill about
2 minutes or until browned lightly.

prep & cook time 10 minutes **makes** 2
nutritional count per toast 1.3g total fat (0.2g
saturated fat); 518kJ (124 cal); 25.2g carbohydrate;
2.8g protein; 2.4g fibre

lemonade ice-blocks

¼ cup (60ml) lemon juice
⅔ cup (110g) icing sugar
1 cup (250ml) sparkling mineral water

1 Stir juice and icing sugar in medium jug until
sugar dissolves. Stir in mineral water.
2 Pour mixture into four ⅓-cup (80ml) ice-block
moulds. Press lids on firmly; freeze 6 hours or
overnight.

prep time 5 minutes (+ freezing) **makes** 4
nutritional count per ice-block 0g total fat (0g
saturated fat); 305kJ (73 cal); 18.6g carbohydrate;
0.1g protein; 0g fibre

the great outdoors

Change the scenery and head outside with these easy-to-transport meals.

tomato, olive and ricotta tart

2 sheets puff pastry
¾ cup (105g) chopped semi-dried tomatoes
¾ cup (90g) seeded black olives
½ cup (120g) crumbled ricotta cheese
½ small red onion (50g), sliced
¼ cup fresh torn basil leaves
1 egg, beaten lightly

1 Preheat oven to 200°C/180°C fan-forced. Line an oven tray with baking paper.
2 Cut a 16cm x 24cm rectangle from one sheet pastry; place on oven tray. Top with tomatoes, olives, cheese, onion and basil leaves.
3 Cut a 18cm x 24cm rectangle from remaining pastry; score pastry in a diamond pattern then place on top of pastry on oven tray, press edges to seal.
4 Brush with egg; bake about 20 minutes.

prep & cook time 35 minutes **serves** 4
nutritional count per serving 25.1g total fat (12.5g saturated fat); 1965kJ (470 cal); 46.9g carbohydrate; 11.5g protein; 5.8g fibre

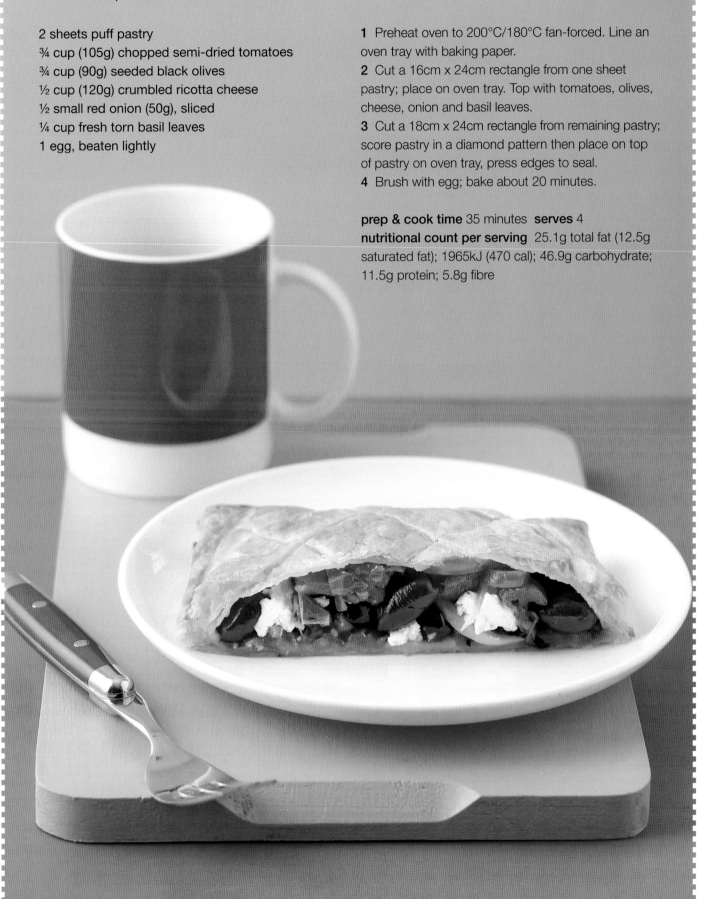

moroccan carrot dip

4 medium carrots (480g), chopped coarsely
2 cloves garlic, peeled
1 teaspoon ground cumin
1 tablespoon honey
2 tablespoons lemon juice
¼ cup (70g) greek-style yogurt
1 tablespoon coarsely chopped fresh
   coriander leaves

1 Cover carrots and garlic with water in small saucepan; bring to the boil. Reduce heat; simmer, covered, 20 minutes or until carrots are soft. Drain.
2 Blend or process carrot mixture with cumin, honey and juice until smooth. Add yogurt; blend until smooth.
3 Serve dip sprinkled with coriander.

prep & cook time 30 minutes **makes** 2 cups
nutritional count per tablespoon 0.2g total fat (0.1g saturated fat); 46kJ (11 cal); 1.9g carbohydrate; 0.3g protein; 0.5g fibre

artichoke spinach dip

340g jar marinated artichokes, rinsed, drained
250g frozen chopped spinach, thawed
½ cup (120g) sour cream
¼ cup (75g) mayonnaise
¾ cup (60g) coarsely grated parmesan cheese
1 clove garlic, crushed

1 Preheat oven to 200°C/180°C fan-forced.
2 Chop artichokes coarsely; combine with remaining ingredients in medium bowl.
3 Transfer dip mixture to 2-cup (500ml) ovenproof dish; cook, covered, 20 minutes.

prep & cook time 30 minutes **makes** 2 cups
nutritional count per tablespoon 2.7g total fat (1.3g saturated fat); 130kJ (31 cal); 0.7g carbohydrate; 1.1g protein; 0.4g fibre

Head outside for a change of scenery and an alfresco feast, then lie back, relax and enjoy the fresh air and sunshine.

smoked trout, brie and cranberry salad

350g trimmed watercress
200g smoked trout, flaked coarsely
110g brie cheese, sliced thinly
cranberry dressing
2 tablespoons olive oil
2 tablespoons cranberry juice
1 tablespoon lemon juice

1 Divide watercress, trout and cheese among serving plates.
2 Make cranberry dressing.
3 Drizzle dressing over salad.
cranberry dressing Place ingredients in screw-top jar; shake well.

prep & cook time 15 minutes **serves** 4
nutritional count per serving 19.8g total fat (7g saturated fat); 1095kJ (262 cal); 1.4g carbohydrate; 19.3g protein; 0.7g fibre

smoked chicken, spinach and almond salad

350g smoked chicken breast fillets, sliced thinly
3 stalks celery (450g), trimmed, sliced thinly
3 small tomatoes (270g), quartered, seeded
100g baby spinach leaves
4 hard-boiled eggs, quartered
2 green onions, sliced thinly
½ cup (70g) slivered almonds, roasted
cumin mayonnaise
2 teaspoons cumin seeds, toasted
½ cup (150g) mayonnaise
¼ cup (60ml) lemon juice

1 Make cumin mayonnaise.
2 Combine chicken, celery, tomato, spinach, egg, onion and nuts in large bowl.
3 Divide salad among serving plates; drizzle over mayonnaise.
cumin mayonnaise Using mortar and pestle, crush seeds finely; combine with mayonnaise and juice in small bowl.

prep & cook time 30 minutes **serves** 4
nutritional count per serving 33.5g total fat (5.3g saturated fat); 2044kJ (489 cal); 11.3g carbohydrate; 34g protein; 4.7g fibre

smoked trout, brie and cranberry salad

smoked chicken, spinach and almond salad

peanut butter cookies

125g butter, softened
¼ cup (70g) crunchy peanut butter
¾ cup (165g) firmly packed brown sugar
1 egg
1½ cups (225g) plain flour
½ teaspoon bicarbonate of soda
½ cup (70g) roasted unsalted peanuts,
 chopped coarsely

1 Preheat oven to 180°C/160°C fan-forced. Grease oven trays; line with baking paper.
2 Beat butter, peanut butter, sugar and egg in small bowl with electric mixer until smooth; do not over-mix. Transfer mixture to medium bowl; stir in sifted flour and soda, then nuts.
3 Roll level tablespoons of mixture into balls; place 5cm apart on trays, flatten with floured fork.
4 Bake cookies about 12 minutes; cool on trays.

prep & cook time 25 minutes **makes** 30
nutritional count per cookie 6g total fat (2.7g saturated fat); 451kJ (108 cal); 11.2g carbohydrate; 2.3g protein; 0.7g fibre

apple slice

1 cup (150g) self-raising flour
½ cup (75g) plain flour
80g cold butter, chopped coarsely
¼ cup (55g) caster sugar
1 egg, beaten lightly
¼ cup (60ml) milk, approximately
1 tablespoon milk, extra
1 tablespoon caster sugar, extra

apple filling
6 medium apples (900g), peeled, cored,
  cut into 1cm pieces
¼ cup (55g) caster sugar
¼ cup (60ml) water
¾ cup (120g) sultanas
1 teaspoon mixed spice
2 teaspoons finely grated lemon rind

1 Make apple filling.
2 Grease 20cm x 30cm lamington pan; line base with baking paper, extending paper 5cm over long sides.
3 Sift flours into medium bowl, rub in butter. Stir in sugar, egg and enough milk to make a firm dough. Knead on floured surface until smooth. Cover; refrigerate 30 minutes.
4 Preheat oven to 200°C/180°C fan-forced.
5 Divide dough in half. Roll one half large enough to cover base of pan; press firmly into pan. Spread apple filling over dough. Roll remaining dough large enough to cover filling and place over the top. Brush with extra milk; sprinkle with extra sugar.
6 Bake slice about 25 minutes; stand in pan 5 minutes.
apple filling Cook apple, sugar and the water in large saucepan, uncovered, stirring occasionally, about 10 minutes or until apple softens. Remove from heat; stir in sultanas, spice and rind. Cool.

prep & cook time 45 minutes (+ refrigeration)
serves 8
nutritional count per serving 9.7g total fat (5.9g saturated fat); 1463kJ (350 cal); 58.6g carbohydrate; 4.8g protein; 3.4g fibre

haloumi and asparagus bites

eggplant fritters

haloumi and asparagus bites

340g asparagus, trimmed
250g haloumi cheese
lemony dressing
1 tablespoon rinsed drained baby capers,
    chopped finely
1 tablespoon olive oil
2 teaspoons finely grated lemon rind
1 tablespoon lemon juice
½ teaspoon white sugar

1 Make lemony dressing.
2 Cut asparagus into 3cm lengths. Boil, steam or microwave until barely tender; rinse under cold water, drain.
3 Cut haloumi into 1cm slices, then into 1cm x 3cm pieces. Thread one piece of asparagus, one piece of haloumi, then another piece of asparagus close together onto each toothpick.
4 Cook bites in large oiled frying pan over high heat about 30 seconds each side or until browned lightly.
5 Serve bites immediately, drizzled with dressing.
lemony dressing Place ingredients in screw-top jar; shake well.

prep & cook time 55 minutes **makes** 40
nutritional count per serving 1.5g total fat (0.8g saturated fat); 88kJ (21 cal); 0.3g carbohydrate; 1.5g protein; 0.1g fibre

eggplant fritters

2 large eggplants (1kg)
1 cup (100g) coarsely grated mozzarella cheese
½ cup coarsely chopped fresh flat-leaf parsley
2 cloves garlic, crushed
½ cup (50g) packaged breadcrumbs
¼ cup (35g) plain flour
2 eggs
vegetable oil, for shallow-frying

1 Preheat oven to 220°C/200°C fan-forced.
2 Remove and discard stem ends from eggplants; prick eggplants all over with fork. Place on oiled oven tray; roast, uncovered, about 30 minutes or until soft. Cool. Peel eggplants; chop flesh finely.
3 Combine eggplant, cheese, parsley, garlic, breadcrumbs, flour and eggs in large bowl. Using wetted hands, shape level tablespoons of mixture into oval patties.
4 Heat oil in large frying pan; cook fritters, in batches, until browned both sides. Drain on absorbent paper. Serve warm or cold, with lemon wedges.

prep & cook time 1 hour **makes** 36
nutritional count per fritter 5.3g total fat (1g saturated fat); 272kJ (65 cal); 2.4g carbohydrate; 1.7g protein; 0.8g fibre

fennel grissini with prosciutto

2 cups (300g) plain flour
½ teaspoon white sugar
1 teaspoon cooking salt
1 teaspoon dried yeast
2 teaspoons fennel seeds
1 cup (250ml) water, approximately
cooking-oil spray
sea salt
20 slices prosciutto (300g)

1 Sift flour, sugar and cooking salt into medium bowl, stir in yeast, seeds and enough of the water to make a soft dough. Turn dough onto floured surface, knead about 5 minutes or until dough is smooth and elastic.
2 Place dough in large oiled bowl, cover with plastic wrap; stand in warm place about 1 hour or until dough is doubled in size.
3 Preheat oven to 220°C/200°C fan-forced. Oil oven trays.
4 Turn dough onto floured surface, knead until smooth. Divide dough into four portions, cut each portion into 15 pieces; roll each piece into a long thin stick.
5 Place sticks on oven trays, coat lightly with oil spray. Sprinkle with sea salt.
6 Bake grissini about 15 minutes or until crisp.
7 Meanwhile, cut each prosciutto slice lengthways into three. Wrap a strip around each warm grissini. Serve immediately.

prep & cook time 1 hour (+ standing) **makes** 60
nutritional count per grissini 0.4g total fat (0.1g saturated fat); 105kJ (25 cal); 3.7g carbohydrate; 1.5g protein; 0.2g fibre

smoked seafood and mixed vegetable antipasti

onion and kumara pakoras with green chilli yogurt

smoked seafood and mixed vegetable antipasti

⅓ cup (80g) sour cream
2 teaspoons raspberry vinegar
1 tablespoon coarsely chopped fresh chives
1 clove garlic, crushed
1 large yellow zucchini (150g)
1 tablespoon raspberry vinegar, extra
¼ cup (60ml) extra virgin olive oil
⅓ cup (45g) roasted slivered almonds
1 cup (150g) drained semi-dried tomatoes
1 large avocado (320g)
1 tablespoon lemon juice
300g hot-smoked ocean trout portions
200g sliced smoked salmon
16 drained caperberries (80g)
1 lemon, cut into wedges
170g packet roasted garlic bagel crisps

1 Combine sour cream, vinegar, chives and garlic in small bowl, cover; refrigerate until required.
2 Meanwhile, using vegetable peeler, slice zucchini lengthways into ribbons; combine zucchini in small bowl with extra vinegar and 2 tablespoons of the oil.
3 Combine nuts, tomatoes and remaining oil in small bowl. Slice avocado thickly into small bowl; sprinkle with juice. Flake trout into bite-sized pieces.
4 Arrange zucchini mixture, nut mixture, avocado, trout, salmon and caperberries on large platter; serve with sour cream mixture, lemon and bagel crisps.

prep time 35 minutes **serves** 4
nutritional count per serving 54.4g total fat (14.1g saturated fat); 3607kJ (863 cal); 44g carbohydrate; 43.2g protein; 10.9g fibre

onion and kumara pakoras with green chilli yogurt

2 cups (300g) chickpea (besan) flour
1 teaspoon ground turmeric
2 teaspoons ground cumin
½ teaspoon chilli powder
1 teaspoon baking powder
½ teaspoon salt
2 teaspoons kalonji seeds
2 medium brown onions (300g), quartered, sliced thinly
1 small uncooked kumara (250g), grated coarsely
1 fresh long green chilli, chopped finely
½ cup (125ml) water, approximately
vegetable oil, for deep-frying
green chilli yogurt
1½ cups (420g) greek-style yogurt
2 fresh long green chillies, seeded, chopped finely
2 tablespoons finely chopped coriander leaves
½ teaspoon ground cumin

1 Sift flour, turmeric, cumin, chilli, baking powder and salt into large bowl. Stir in seeds, onion, kumara and chilli. Gradually stir in enough water to make a thick batter.
2 Make green chilli yogurt.
3 Heat oil in wok or deep wide saucepan; deep-fry rounded teaspoons of batter mixture, in batches, until browned. Drain on absorbent paper.
4 Serve pakoras hot, with yogurt.
green chilli yogurt Combine ingredients in medium bowl.

prep & cook time 35 minutes **makes** 80
nutritional count per pakora 1.2g total fat (0.4g saturated fat); 121kJ (29 cal); 2g carbohydrate; 2.2g protein; 0.6g fibre

There's no work involved in eating these delicious little crabs – no need to crack, dig and pick to get to the flesh.

tip Don't be put off by the idea of consuming the whole crab – soft-shell crab is considered by many to be one of the greatest seafood delicacies. The shells are paper thin and slightly crunchy, like a potato crisp.

soft-shell crabs with green onion aïoli

½ cup (100g) rice flour
1 teaspoon dried chilli flakes
2 teaspoons sea salt
8 uncooked small soft-shell crabs (500g)
vegetable oil, for deep-frying
1 cup loosely packed fresh basil leaves
green onion aïoli
¾ cup (225g) mayonnaise
2 green onions, sliced finely
1 clove garlic, crushed
1 tablespoon lemon juice

1 Make green onion aïoli.
2 Combine flour, chilli and salt in medium bowl.
3 Clean crabs; pat dry then cut into quarters. Coat crabs with flour mixture; shake away excess.
4 Heat oil in large saucepan; deep-fry basil about 30 seconds or until crisp. Drain on absorbent paper. Deep-fry crabs, in batches, until browned lightly. Drain on absorbent paper. Serve with basil and aïoli.
green onion aïoli Combine ingredients in small bowl.

prep & cook time 30 minutes **serves** 8
nutritional count per serving 13g total fat (1.5g saturated fat); 920kJ (220 cal); 16.7g carbohydrate; 9g protein; 0.6g fibre

These brightly coloured little terrines are just as impressive to eat as they are to look at, and can be made well in advance.

roasted capsicum and goats cheese terrines

3 large red capsicums (1kg)
1½ cups (360g) ricotta cheese, chopped coarsely
250g firm goats cheese, chopped coarsely
¼ cup finely chopped fresh chives
2 tablespoons lemon juice
1 clove garlic, crushed
spinach and walnut pesto
¼ cup (20g) finely grated parmesan cheese
100g baby spinach leaves
¼ cup (25g) roasted walnuts
1 clove garlic, quartered
¼ cup (60ml) olive oil
2 tablespoons lemon juice
1 tablespoon water

1 Preheat oven to 240°C/220°C fan-forced. Grease six holes of eight-hole (½-cup/125ml) petite loaf pan. Line base and two long sides of each hole with a strip of baking paper, extending 5cm over sides.
2 Halve capsicums; discard seeds and membranes. Place on oven tray; roast, skin-side up, 15 minutes or until skin blisters and blackens. Cover with plastic wrap for 5 minutes then peel away skin. Cut capsicum into strips; line base and two long sides of pan holes with capsicum strips, extending 2cm over edges.
3 Combine remaining ingredients in medium bowl; spoon cheese mixture into pan holes, pressing down firmly. Fold capsicum strips over to enclose filling. Cover; refrigerate 1 hour.
4 Meanwhile, make spinach and walnut pesto.
5 Carefully remove terrines from pan holes; serve with spinach and walnut pesto. Sprinkle with chopped fresh chives.
spinach and walnut pesto Process cheese, spinach, nuts and garlic until chopped finely. With motor operating, gradually add combined oil, juice and the water in a thin, steady stream; process until pesto is smooth.

prep & cook time 45 minutes (+ refrigeration)
makes 6
nutritional count per terrine 26.8g total fat (10.8g saturated fat); 1417kJ (339 cal); 7.5g carbohydrate; 16.5g protein; 2.6g fibre

crostini with fetta, artichokes and rocket

olive oil spray
1 small french bread (150g), cut into 8mm-thick slices
1 clove garlic, halved
30g baby rocket leaves
1 teaspoon extra virgin olive oil
1 teaspoon red wine vinegar
5 marinated drained artichoke hearts
100g fetta cheese, crumbled

1 Preheat oven to 180°C/160°C fan-forced.
2 Spray both sides bread slices with oil spray; place on oven tray, toast in oven. Rub one side of each crostini with cut side of garlic clove; place crostini on serving platter.
3 Combine rocket leaves, oil and vinegar in medium bowl. Cut each artichoke heart into six wedges.
4 Top crostini with rocket mixture, then artichokes; sprinkle with fetta and freshly ground black pepper.

prep & cook time 20 minutes **serves** 6
nutritional count per serving 5.7g total fat (2.8g saturated fat); 548kJ (131 cal); 13.6g carbohydrate; 5.6g protein; 1.4g fibre

Two of the best things in life are good food and good friends — so bring them together, pour out the bubbly and chink your glasses.

Lamb cutlets are perfect stand-up party food — ready to pick up and eat with their own natural 'handle' to hold.

lamb cutlets with spinach skordalia

2 tablespoons olive oil
2 tablespoons lemon juice
2 cloves garlic, crushed
2 teaspoons dried oregano
18 french-trimmed small lamb cutlets (900g)
spinach skordalia
¾ cup (50g) stale breadcrumbs
⅓ cup (80ml) water
1kg spinach, trimmed, chopped coarsely
¾ cup (75g) roasted walnuts
2 cloves garlic, chopped coarsely
¼ cup (60ml) lemon juice
¼ cup (60ml) olive oil

1 Combine oil, juice, garlic and oregano with lamb in large bowl. Cover; refrigerate 1 hour.
2 Meanwhile, make spinach skordalia.
3 Cook lamb, in batches, on heated oiled grill plate (or grill or barbecue) until browned both sides and cooked as desired.
4 Serve cutlets with skordalia.

spinach skordalia Combine breadcrumbs and the water in small bowl. Drop spinach into large saucepan of boiling water; drain, rinse immediately under cold water, drain. Squeeze spinach to extract any excess water. Blend or process spinach and breadcrumb mixture with nuts, garlic and juice until smooth. With motor operating, gradually add oil in a thin steady stream; process until skordalia thickens.

prep & cook time 30 minutes (+ refrigeration)
serves 6
nutritional count per serving 37.5g total fat (8.6g saturated fat); 1944kJ (465 cal); 7.7g carbohydrate; 22.3g protein; 6g fibre

roasted eye fillet with rösti and mushrooms

2 tablespoons olive oil
800g beef eye fillet
1 large kumara (500g)
2 large russet burbank potatoes (600g)
80g butter
2 tablespoons olive oil, extra
30g butter, extra
200g swiss brown mushrooms, halved
200g enoki mushrooms, trimmed
150g oyster mushrooms, halved
200g crème fraîche
3 green onions, sliced thinly
⅓ cup firmly packed fresh flat-leaf parsley

1 Preheat oven to 220°C/200°C fan-forced.
2 Heat oil in large shallow flameproof baking dish; cook beef, uncovered, until browned all over. Roast, uncovered, about 35 minutes or until cooked as desired. Cover to keep warm.
3 Meanwhile, coarsely grate kumara and potatoes into large bowl. Using hands, squeeze out excess moisture from potato mixture; shape mixture into eight portions. Heat 10g of the butter and 1 teaspoon of the extra oil in medium non-stick frying pan; spread one portion of the potato mixture over base of pan, flatten with spatula to form a firm pancake-like rösti. Cook, uncovered, over medium heat until browned; invert rösti onto large plate then gently slide back into pan to cook other side. Drain on absorbent paper; cover to keep warm. Repeat process with remaining butter, oil and potato mixture.
4 Heat extra butter in same cleaned pan; cook mushrooms, stirring, until just tender. Add crème fraîche; bring to the boil. Reduce heat; simmer, stirring, until sauce thickens slightly. Remove from heat; stir in onion and parsley.
5 Serve sliced beef with rösti and mushrooms.

prep & cook time 1 hour 10 minutes **serves** 4
nutritional count per serving 69.9g total fat (34.1g saturated fat); 4080kJ (976 cal); 34.4g carbohydrate; 54.2g protein; 8.4g fibre

chocolate and raspberry tart

¾ cup (240g) raspberry jam
200g dark eating chocolate, chopped finely
25g unsalted butter, melted
⅔ cup (160ml) cream, warmed
120g raspberries
sweet pastry
1¼ cups (185g) plain flour
½ cup (80g) icing sugar
125g cold unsalted butter, chopped coarsely
¼ cup (60ml) iced water, approximately

1 Make sweet pastry.
2 Grease 12.5cm x 35cm (or 24cm-round) loose-based flan tin. Roll pastry between sheets of baking paper until large enough to line tin. Ease pastry into tin, press into base and side; trim edge, prick base with fork. Cover; refrigerate 30 minutes.
3 Preheat oven to 200°C/180°C fan-forced.

4 Place tin on oven tray; cover pastry with baking paper, fill with dried beans or uncooked rice. Bake 15 minutes; remove paper and beans carefully from pastry case. Bake about 10 minutes. Spread jam over pastry base; return to oven 2 minutes. Cool.
5 Whisk chocolate, butter and cream in medium bowl until smooth. Pour chocolate mixture into pastry case; refrigerate 2 hours. Top tart with raspberries.
sweet pastry Process flour, icing sugar and butter until crumbly; add enough of the water to make ingredients come together. Knead dough gently on floured surface until smooth. Wrap in plastic; refrigerate 30 minutes.

prep & cook time 45 minutes (+ refrigeration)
serves 12
nutritional count per serving 21g total fat (13.4g saturated fat); 1559kJ (373 cal); 42.4g carbohydrate; 3g protein; 1.6g fibre

orange-poached pears

6 medium pears (1.4kg)
2 cups (500ml) water
2 cups (500ml) dry red wine
2 tablespoons orange-flavoured liqueur
¾ cup (165g) caster sugar
1 teaspoon vanilla bean paste
4 x 5cm strips orange rind
⅓ cup (80ml) orange juice

1 Peel pears, leaving stems intact.
2 Place the remaining ingredients in large saucepan; stir over heat, without boiling, until sugar dissolves. Add pears; bring to the boil. Reduce heat; simmer, covered, about 1 hour or until pears are tender.
3 Transfer pears to serving bowls.
4 Bring syrup in pan to the boil. Boil, uncovered, about 10 minutes or until syrup thickens slightly. Serve pears drizzled with warm syrup.

prep & cook time 1 hour 20 minutes **serves** 6
nutritional count per serving 0.2g total fat (0g saturated fat); 1317kJ (315 cal); 57.1g carbohydrate; 0.8g protein; 3.5g fibre

glossary

allspice also called pimento or jamaican pepper; tastes like a combination of nutmeg, cumin, clove and cinnamon. Available whole or ground.

almonds

blanched brown skins removed.

flaked paper-thin slices.

meal also called ground almonds.

slivered small pieces cut lengthways.

bacon also called bacon slices.

baking powder a raising agent consisting mainly of two parts cream of tartar to one part bicarbonate of soda.

bay leaves aromatic leaves from the bay tree, fresh or dried; adds a strong, slightly peppery flavour.

beans

black-eyed also known as black-eyed peas or cowpea; the dried seed of a variant of the snake or yard-long bean. Not too dissimilar to white beans in flavour; good cooked and used cold in salads.

borlotti also called roman beans or pink beans, can be eaten fresh or dried. Interchangeable with pinto beans due to their similarity in appearance – pale pink or beige with dark red streaks.

broad also called fava, windsor and horse beans; available dried, fresh, canned and frozen. Fresh should be peeled twice (discard the outer long green pod and the beige-green tough inner shell); the frozen beans have had their pods removed but the beige shell still needs removal.

cannellini small white bean similar in appearance and flavour to other *Phaseolus vulgaris* varieties (great northern, navy or haricot). Available dried or canned.

kidney medium-size red bean, slightly floury in texture yet sweet in flavour; sold dried or canned, it's found in bean mixes and is used in chilli con carne.

lima large, flat kidney-shaped, beige dried and canned beans. Also known as butter beans.

pinto similar to borlotti, a plump, kidney-shaped, pinky-beige bean speckled with brown to red streaks; available canned or dried and used in Mexican cooking.

snake long (about 40cm), thin, round, fresh green beans, Asian in origin, with a taste similar to green or french beans. Used most frequently in stir-fries, they are also called yard-long beans because of their (pre-metric) length.

sprouts also called bean shoots; tender new growths of assorted beans and seeds germinated for consumption as sprouts. Sprout mixtures or tendrils are also available.

beef

corned beef also called corned silverside; little fat, cut from the upper leg and cured. Sold cryovac-packed in brine.

eye-fillet tenderloin, fillet; fine texture, most expensive and extremely tender.

beetroot also called red beets; firm, round root vegetable.

bicarbonate of soda also called baking soda.

breadcrumbs

packaged prepared fine-textured but crunchy white breadcrumbs; good for coating foods that are to be fried.

stale crumbs made by grating, blending or processing 1- or 2-day-old bread.

brioche French in origin; a rich, yeast-leavened, cake-like bread made with butter and eggs. Available from cake or specialty bread shops.

broccolini a cross between broccoli and Chinese kale; long asparagus-like stems with a long loose floret, both completely edible. Resembles broccoli but is milder and sweeter in taste.

butter we use salted butter unless stated otherwise; 125g is equal to 1 stick (4 ounces).

butter lettuce small, round, loosely formed heads with a sweet flavour; soft, buttery-textured leaves range from pale green on the outer leaves to pale yellow-green inner leaves.

buttermilk in spite of its name, buttermilk is actually low in fat. Originally the term given to the slightly sour liquid left after butter was churned from cream, today it is intentionally made from no-fat or low-fat milk with specific bacterial cultures added during manufacturing. It is readily available from the dairy department in supermarkets. Because it is low in fat, it's a good substitute for dairy products like cream or sour cream in some baking and salad dressings.

caperberries olive-sized fruit formed after the buds of the caper bush have flowered; they are usually sold pickled in a vinegar brine with stalks intact.

capers grey-green buds of a Mediterranean shrub, sold either dried and salted or pickled in a vinegar brine; tiny young ones, called baby capers, are also available both in brine or dried in salt. Their pungent taste adds piquancy to a classic steak tartare, tapenade, sauces and condiments.

capsicum also called pepper or bell pepper. Discard seeds and membranes before use.

caraway seeds the small, half-moon-shaped dried seed from a member of the parsley family; adds a sharp anise flavour when used in both sweet and savoury dishes. Used widely, in foods such as rye bread, harissa and the classic Hungarian fresh cheese, liptauer.

cardamom a spice native to India and used extensively in its cuisine; can be purchased in pod, seed or ground form. Has a distinctive aromatic, sweetly rich flavour and is one of the world's most expensive spices.

cashews plump, kidney-shaped, golden-brown nuts with a distinctive sweet, buttery flavour; conts about 48 per cent fat. Due to their high fat content, they should be kept, sealed, in the refrigerator to avoid becoming rancid. We use roasted unsalted cashews unless otherwise stated; they're available from health-food stores and most supermarkets. Roasting cashews brings out their intense nutty flavour.

cayenne pepper a thin-fleshed, long, extremely hot dried red chilli, usually purchased ground.

cheese

blue mould-treated cheeses mottled with blue veining. Varieties include firm and crumbly stilton types and mild, creamy brie-like cheeses.

bocconcini from the diminutive of "boccone", meaning mouthful in Italian; walnut-sized, baby mozzarella, a delicate, semi-soft, white cheese traditionally made from buffalo milk. Sold fresh, it spoils rapidly so will only keep, refrigerated in brine, for 1 or 2 days at the most.

fetta Greek in origin; a crumbly textured goat- or sheep-milk cheese having a sharp, salty taste. Ripened and stored in salted whey; particularly good cubed and tossed into salads.

fontina a smooth, firm Italian cow-milk cheese with a creamy, nutty taste and brown or red rind; an ideal melting or grilling cheese.

gorgonzola a creamy Italian blue cheese with a mild, sweet taste; good as an accompaniment to fruit or used to flavour sauces.

gruyère a hard-rind Swiss cheese with small holes and a nutty, slightly salty flavour. A popular cheese for soufflés.

haloumi a Greek Cypriot cheese with a semi-firm, spongy texture and very salty sweet flavour. Ripened and stored in salted whey; best grilled or fried, and holds its shape well on being heated. Eat while still warm as it becomes tough and rubbery on cooling.

mascarpone an Italian fresh cultured-cream product made in much the same way as yogurt. White to creamy yellow in colour, with a buttery-rich, luscious texture. Soft, creamy and spreadable, it is used in Italian desserts and as an accompaniment to fresh fruit.

mozzarella soft, spun-curd cheese; originating in southern Italy where it was traditionally made from water-buffalo milk. Now generally made from cow milk, it is the most popular pizza cheese because of its low melting point and elasticity when heated.

parmesan also called parmigiano; is a hard, grainy cow-milk cheese originating in the Parma region of Italy. The curd for this cheese is salted in brine for a month, then aged for up to 2 years in humid conditions. Reggiano is the best parmesan, aged for a minimum 2 years and made only in the Italian region of Emilia-Romagna.

ricotta a soft, sweet, moist, white cow-milk cheese with a low fat content (8.5 per cent) and a slightly grainy texture. The name roughly translates as "cooked again" and refers to ricotta's manufacture from a whey that is itself a by-product of other cheese making.

chervil also known as cicily; mildly fennel-flavoured member of the parsley family with curly dark-green leaves. Available both fresh and dried but, like all herbs, is best used fresh; like coriander and parsley, its delicate flavour diminishes the longer it's cooked.

chicken

barbecued we use cooked whole barbecued chickens about 900g each in our recipes. Skin discarded and bones removed, this size chicken provides about 4 cups (400g) shredded meat or 3 cups (400g) coarsely chopped meat.

breast fillet breast halved, skinned and boned.

thigh skin and bone intact.

thigh cutlet thigh with skin and centre bone intact; sometimes found skinned with bone intact.

thigh fillet thigh with skin and centre bone removed.

chilli

powder the Asian variety is the hottest, made from dried ground thai chillies; can be used instead of fresh in the proportion of ½ teaspoon chilli powder to 1 medium chopped fresh red chilli.

thai also known as "scuds"; tiny, very hot and bright red in colour.

chinese cooking wine Chinese cooking wine also called hao hsing or chinese rice wine; made from fermented rice, wheat, sugar and salt with a 13.5 per cent alcohol content. Inexpensive and found in Asian food shops; if you can't find it, replace with mirin or sherry.

chipolata sausages also known as 'little fingers'; highly spiced, coarse-textured beef sausage.

chocolate

Choc Bits also known as chocolate chips or chocolate morsels; available in milk, white and dark chocolate. Made of cocoa liquor, cocoa butter, sugar and an emulsifier, these hold their shape in baking and are ideal for decorating.

dark eating also called semi-sweet or luxury chocolate; made of a high percentage of cocoa liquor and cocoa butter, and little added sugar. Unless stated otherwise, we use dark eating chocolate as it's ideal for use in desserts and cakes.

milk most popular eating chocolate, mild and very sweet; similar in make-up to dark with the difference being the addition of milk solids.

white contains no cocoa solids but derives its sweet flavour from cocoa butter. Very sensitive to heat.

chocolate hazelnut spread also known as Nutella; made of cocoa powder, hazelnuts, sugar and milk.

chorizo sausage of Spanish origin, made of coarsely ground pork and highly seasoned with garlic and chilli.

choy sum also called pakaukeo or flowering cabbage, a member of the buk choy family; easy to identify with its long stems, light green leaves and yellow flowers. Stems and leaves are both edible, steamed or stir-fried.

cinnamon available both in pieces (called sticks or quills) and ground into powder; one of the world's most common spices, it is used universally as a sweet, fragrant flavouring for both sweet and savoury foods.

cloves dried flower buds of a tropical tree; can be used whole or in ground form. They have a strong scent and taste so should be used sparingly.

cocoa powder also known as unsweetened cocoa.

coconut

desiccated concentrated, dried, unsweetened and finely shredded coconut flesh.

flaked dried flaked coconut flesh.

milk not the liquid found inside the fruit, which is called coconut water, but the diluted liquid from the second pressing of the white flesh of a mature coconut (the first pressing produces coconut cream). Available in cans and cartons at most supermarkets.

shredded unsweetened thin strips of dried coconut flesh.

coffee-flavoured liqueur such as kahlua.

cornflour also called cornstarch. Available made from corn or wheat (wheaten cornflour, gluten-free, gives a lighter texture in cakes); used as a thickening agent in cooking.

cornichon French for gherkin, a very small variety of cucumber. Pickled, they are a traditional accompaniment to pâté; the Swiss always serve them with fondue (or raclette).

cos lettuce also called romaine lettuce; the traditional caesar salad lettuce. Long, with leaves ranging from dark green on the outside to almost white near the core; the leaves have a stiff centre rib giving a slight cupping effect to the leaf on either side.

couscous a fine, grain-like cereal product made from semolina; from the countries of North Africa. A semolina flour and water dough is sieved then dehydrated to produce minuscule even-sized pellets of couscous; it is rehydrated by steaming or with the addition of a warm liquid and swells to three or four times its original size; eaten like rice with a tagine, as a side dish or salad ingredient.

cranberries available fresh and frozen; have a rich, astringent flavour and can be used in cooking sweet and savoury dishes.

dried sweetened and dried cranberries; used in cooking sweet or savoury dishes. Can usually be substituted for or with other dried fruit in most recipes.

cream

pouring also called pure cream. It has no additives, and contains a minimum fat content of 35 per cent.

thickened a whipping cream that contains a thickener; a minimum fat content of 35 per cent.

cream of tartar the acid ingredient in baking powder; added to confectionery mixtures to help prevent sugar from crystallising. Keeps frostings creamy and improves volume when beating egg whites.

crème fraîche a mature, naturally fermented cream (minimum fat content 35 per cent) having a velvety texture and slightly tangy, nutty flavour. Crème fraîche, a French variation of sour cream, can boil without curdling and be used in sweet and savoury dishes.

cumin also known as zeera or comino; resembling caraway in size, cumin is the dried seed of a plant related to the parsley family. Its spicy, almost curry-like flavour is essential to the traditional foods of Mexico, India, North Africa and the Middle East. Available dried as seeds or ground.

custard powder instant mixture used to make pouring custard;

similar to North American instant pudding mixes.

dates fruit of the date palm tree, eaten fresh or dried, on their own or in prepared dishes. About 4cm to 6cm in length, oval and plump, thin-skinned, with a honey-sweet flavour and sticky texture.

dried chinese sausage also called lap cheong; highly spiced, bright red, thin pork sausages. The meat is preserved by the high spice content and can be kept at room temperature.

dried currants tiny, almost black raisins so-named after a grape variety that originated in Corinth, Greece.

duck we use whole ducks in some recipes; available from specialty chicken shops, open-air markets and some supermarkets.

breast fillets boneless whole breasts, with the skin on.

chinese barbecued traditionally cooked in special ovens in China; dipped into and brushed during roasting with a sticky sweet coating made from soy sauce, sherry, ginger, five-spice, star anise and hoisin sauce. Available from Asian food shops as well as dedicated Chinese barbecued meat shops.

eggplant also called aubergine; often thought of as a vegetable but actually a fruit and belongs to the same family as the tomato, chilli and potato. ranging in size from tiny to very large and in colour from pale green to deep purple. can be purchased char-grilled, packed in oil, in jars.

eggs if a recipe calls for raw or barely cooked eggs, exercise caution if there is a salmonella problem in your area, particularly in food eaten by children and pregnant women.

fennel also called finocchio or anise; a crunchy green vegetable slightly resembling celery that's eaten raw in salads; fried as an accompaniment; or used as an ingredient in soups and sauces. Also the name given to the dried seeds of the plant which have a stronger licorice flavour.

flour

buckwheat a herb in the same plant family as rhubarb; not a cereal so it is gluten-free. Available as flour; ground (cracked) into coarse, medium or fine granules (kasha) and used similarly to polenta; or groats, the whole kernel sold roasted as a cereal product.

chickpea (besan) made from ground chickpeas so is gluten-free and high in protein. Used in Indian cooking to make dumplings, noodles and chapati; for a batter coating for deep-frying; and as a sauce thickener.

plain also known as all-purpose; unbleached wheat flour is the best for baking: the gluten content ensures a strong dough, which produces a light result.

rice very fine, almost powdery, gluten-free flour; made from ground white rice. Used in baking, as a thickener, and in some Asian noodles and desserts. Another variety, made from glutinous sweet rice, is used for chinese dumplings and rice paper.

self-raising all-purpose plain or wholemeal flour with baking powder and salt added; make yourself with plain or wholemeal flour sifted with baking powder in the proportion of 1 cup flour to 2 teaspoons baking powder.

gai lan also known as gai larn, chinese broccoli and chinese kale; green vegetable appreciated more for its stems than its coarse leaves. Can be served steamed and stir-fried, in soups and noodle dishes. One of the most popular Asian greens, best known for its appearance on a yum cha trolley, where it's steamed then sprinkled with a mixture of oyster sauce and sesame oil.

gelatine we use dried (powdered) gelatine in this book; it's also available in sheet form known as leaf gelatine. A thickening agent made from either collagen, a protein found in animal connective tissue and bones, or certain algae (agar-agar). Three teaspoons of dried gelatine (8g or one sachet) is about the same as four gelatine leaves. The two types are interchangable but leaf gelatine gives a much clearer mixture than dried gelatine; it's perfect in dishes where appearance matters.

ginger

fresh also called green or root ginger; the thick gnarled root of a tropical plant. Store, peeled, covered with dry sherry in a jar and refrigerated, or frozen in an airtight container.

ground also called powdered ginger; cannot be substituted for fresh ginger.

golden syrup a by-product of refined sugarcane; pure maple syrup or honey can be substituted. Golden syrup and treacle (a thicker, darker syrup not unlike molasses), also known as flavour syrups, are similar sugar products made by partly breaking down sugar into its component parts and adding water. Treacle is more viscous, and has a stronger flavour and aroma than golden syrup (which has been refined further and contains fewer impurities, so is lighter in colour and more fluid).

Both can be use in baking and for making certain confectionery items.

hazelnuts also known as filberts; plump, grape-sized, rich, sweet nut having a brown skin that is removed by rubbing heated nuts together vigorously in a tea-towel.

meal is made by grounding the hazelnuts to a coarse flour texture for use in baking or as a thickening agent.

hazelnut-flavoured liqueur such as frangelico.

honey the variety sold in a squeezable container is not suitable for the recipes in this book.

horseradish a vegetable with edible green leaves but mainly grown for its long, pungent white root. Occasionally found fresh in specialty greengrocers and some Asian food shops, but commonly purchased in bottles at the supermarket in two forms: prepared horseradish and horseradish cream. These cannot be substituted one for the other in cooking but both can be used as table condiments. Horseradish cream is a commercially prepared creamy paste consisting of grated horseradish, vinegar, oil and sugar, while prepared horseradish is the preserved grated root.

kaffir lime leaves also known as bai magrood and looks like two glossy dark green leaves joined end to end, forming a rounded hourglass shape. Used fresh or dried in many South-East Asian dishes, they are used like bay leaves or curry leaves, especially in Thai cooking. Sold fresh, dried or frozen, the dried leaves are less potent so double the number if using them as a substitute for fresh; a strip of fresh lime peel may be substituted for each kaffir lime leaf.

kalonji also called nigella or black onion seeds. Tiny, angular seeds, black on the outside and creamy within, with a sharp nutty flavour that is enhanced by frying briefly in a dry hot pan before use. Typically sprinkled over Turkish bread immediately after baking or as an important spice in Indian cooking, kalonji can be found in most Asian and Middle Eastern food shops. Often erroneously called black cumin seeds.

kecap asin a thick, dark, salty Indonesian soy sauce.

kecap manis a dark, thick sweet soy sauce used in most South-East Asian cuisines. Depending on the manufacturer, the sauces's sweetness is derived from the addition of either molasses or palm sugar when brewed.

kumara the polynesian name of an orange-fleshed sweet potato often confused with yam; good baked, boiled, mashed or fried similarly to other potatoes.

lamb

backstrap also known as eye of loin; the larger fillet from a row of loin chops or cutlets. Tender, best cooked rapidly: barbecued or pan-fried.

shank forequarter leg; sometimes sold as drumsticks or frenched shanks if the gristle and narrow end of the bone are discarded and the remaining meat trimmed.

lebanese cucumbers short, slender and thin-skinned. Probably the most popular variety because of its tender, edible skin, tiny, yielding seeds, and sweet, fresh and flavoursome taste.

leeks a member of the onion family, the leek resembles a green onion but is much larger and more subtle in flavour. Tender baby or pencil leeks can be eaten whole with minimal cooking but adult leeks are usually trimmed of most of the green tops then chopped or sliced and cooked as an ingredient in stews, casseroles and soups.

lemon grass also known as takrai, serai or serah. A tall, clumping, lemon-smelling and tasting, sharp-edged aromatic tropical grass; the white lower part of the stem is used, finely chopped, in much of the cooking of South-East Asia. Can be found, fresh, dried, powdered and frozen, in supermarkets, greengrocers and Asian food shops.

lychees a small fruit from China with a hard shell and sweet, juicy flesh. The white flesh has a gelatinous texture and musky, perfumed taste. Discard the rough skin and seed before using in salads or as a dessert fruit. Also available canned in a sugar syrup.

maple-flavoured syrup is made from sugar cane and is also known as golden or pancake syrup. It is not a substitute for pure maple syrup.

maple syrup distilled from the sap of sugar maple trees found only in Canada and about ten states in the USA. Most often eaten with pancakes or waffles, but also used as an ingredient in baking or in preparing desserts. Maple-flavoured syrup or pancake syrup is not an adequate substitute for the real thing.

mayonnaise, whole-egg high quality commercial mayonnaise made with whole eggs and labelled as such; some mayonnaises substitute emulsifiers such as food starch, cellulose gel or other thickeners to achieve the same thick and creamy consistency but never achieve the same rich flavour. Must be refrigerated once opened.

milk we use full-cream homogenised milk unless stated otherwise.

evaporated unsweetened canned milk from which water has been extracted by evaporation. Evaporated skim or low-fat milk has 0.3 per cent fat content.

sweetened condensed a canned milk product consisting of milk with more than half the water content removed and sugar added to the remaining milk.

mixed dried fruit a combination of sultanas, raisins, currants, mixed peel and cherries.

mixed spice a classic spice mixture generally containing caraway, allspice, coriander, cumin, nutmeg and ginger, although cinnamon and other spices can be added. It is used with fruit and in cakes.

mushrooms

button small, cultivated white mushrooms with a mild flavour. When a recipe in this book calls for an unspecified type of mushroom, use button.

enoki also known as enokitake; grown and bought in clumps, these delicately-flavoured mushrooms have small cream caps on long thin stalks. Available from Asian food shops and most supermarkets.

flat large, flat mushrooms with a rich earthy flavour, ideal for filling and barbecuing. They are sometimes misnamed field mushrooms which are wild mushrooms.

oyster also known as abalone; grey-white mushrooms shaped like a fan. Prized for their smooth texture and subtle, oyster-like flavour.

shiitake fresh, are also known as Chinese black, forest or golden oak mushrooms. Although cultivated, they have the earthiness

and taste of wild mushrooms. Large and meaty, they can be used as a substitute for meat in some Asian vegetarian dishes. dried also called donko or dried Chinese mushrooms; have a unique meaty flavour. Sold dried; rehydrate before use.

swiss brown also known as roman or cremini. Light to dark brown mushrooms with full-bodied flavour; suited for use in casseroles or being stuffed and baked.

mustard

dijon also called french. Pale brown, creamy, distinctively flavoured, fairly mild French mustard.

powder finely ground white (yellow) mustard seeds.

wholegrain also known as seeded. A French-style coarse-grain mustard made from crushed mustard seeds and dijon-style french mustard. Works well with cold meats and sausages.

noodles

dried rice noodles also known as rice stick noodles. Made from rice flour and water, available flat and wide or very thin (vermicelli). Must be soaked in boiling water to soften.

fresh rice also called ho fun, khao pun, sen yau, pho or kway tiau, depending on the country of manufacture; the most common form of noodle used in Thailand. Can be purchased in strands of various widths or large sheets weighing about 500g which are to be cut into the desired noodle size. Chewy and pure white, they do not need pre-cooking before use.

hokkien also known as stir-fry noodles; fresh wheat noodles resembling thick, yellow-brown spaghetti needing no pre-cooking before use.

rice stick also known as sen lek, ho fun or kway teow; especially popular South-East Asian dried rice noodles. They come in different widths (thin used in soups, wide in stir-fries), but all should be soaked in hot water to soften. The traditional noodle used in pad thai which, before soaking, measures about 5mm in width.

rice vermicelli also known as sen mee, mei fun or bee hoon. Used throughout Asia in spring rolls and cold salads; similar to bean threads, only longer and made with rice flour instead of mung bean starch. Before using, soak the dried noodles in hot water until softened, boil them briefly then rinse with hot water. Vermicelli can also be deep-fried until crunchy and used in salad or as a garnish or bed for sauces.

nutmeg a strong and pungent spice ground from the dried nut of an evergreen tree native to Indonesia. Usually found ground but the flavour is more intense from a whole nut, available from spice shops, so it's best to grate your own. Used most often in baking and milk-based desserts, but also works nicely in savoury dishes. Found in mixed spice mixtures.

oil

cooking spray we use a cholesterol-free cooking spray made from canola oil.

olive made from ripened olives. Extra virgin and virgin are the first and second press, respectively, of the olives and are therefore considered the best; the "extra light" or "light" name on other types refers to taste not fat levels.

peanut pressed from ground peanuts; the most commonly used oil in Asian cooking because of its high smoke point (capacity to handle high heat without burning).

sesame made from roasted, crushed, white sesame seeds; a flavouring rather than a cooking medium.

vegetable any number of oils from plant rather than animal fats.

onions

brown and white are interchangeable. Their pungent flesh adds flavour to a vast range of dishes.

green also known as scallion or (incorrectly) shallot; an immature onion picked before the bulb has formed, having a long, bright-green edible stalk.

red also known as spanish, red spanish or bermuda onion; a sweet-flavoured, large, purple-red onion.

spring crisp, narrow green-leafed tops and a round sweet white bulb larger than green onions.

orange-flavoured liqueur such as grand marnier and cointreau.

pancetta an Italian unsmoked bacon, pork belly cured in salt and spices then rolled into a sausage shape and dried for several weeks. Used, sliced or chopped, as an ingredient rather than eaten on its own; can also be used to add taste and moisture to tough or dry cuts of meat.

paprika ground dried sweet red capsicum (bell pepper); grades and types available include sweet, hot, mild and smoked.

peanuts also called groundnut, not in fact a nut but the pod of a legume. We use raw (unroasted) or roasted unsalted peanuts.

pecans native to the US and now grown locally; pecans are golden brown, buttery and rich. Good in savoury as well as sweet dishes; walnuts are a good substitute.

pine nuts also known as pignoli; not a nut but a small, cream-coloured kernel from pine cones. They are best roasted before use to bring out the flavour.

pistachios green, delicately flavoured nuts inside hard off-white shells. Available salted or unsalted in their shells; you can also get them shelled.

polenta also known as cornmeal; a flour-like cereal made of dried corn (maize). Also the name of the dish made from it.

potatoes

desiree oval, smooth and pink-skinned, waxy yellow flesh; good in salads, boiled and roasted.

kipfler small, finger-shaped, nutty flavour; great baked and in salads.

new potatoes also known as chats; not a separate variety but an early harvest with very thin skin. Good unpeeled steamed, eaten hot or cold in salads.

russet burbank long and oval, rough white skin with shallow eyes, white flesh; good for baking and frying.

prosciutto a kind of unsmoked Italian ham; salted, air-cured and aged, it is usually eaten uncooked. There are many styles of prosciutto, one of the best being Parma ham, from Italy's Emilia Romagna region, traditionally lightly salted, dried then eaten raw.

puff pastry packaged sheets of frozen puff pastry, available from supermarkets.

radicchio Italian in origin; a member of the chicory family. The dark burgundy leaves and strong, bitter flavour can be cooked or eaten raw in salads.

rhubarb a plant with long, green-red stalks; becomes sweet and edible when cooked.

rice

arborio small, round grain rice well-suited to absorb a large amount of liquid; the high level of starch makes it especially suitable for risottos, giving the dish its classic creaminess.

basmati a white, fragrant long-grained rice; the grains fluff up beautifully when cooked. It should be washed several times before cooking.

calasparra a short-grained rice available from Spanish delicatessens and gourmet-food stores. If you can't find calasparra, any short-graine rice can be substituted.

jasmine or Thai jasmine, is a long-grained white rice recognised around the world as having a perfumed aromatic quality; moist in texture, it clings together after cooking. Sometimes substituted for basmati rice.

koshihikari small, round-grain white rice. Substitute white short-grain rice and cook by the absorption method.

long-grain elongated grains that remain separate when cooked; this is the most popular steaming rice in Asia.

short-grain fat, almost round grain with a high starch content; tends to clump together when cooked.

white is hulled and polished rice, can be short-or long-grained.

rocket also called arugula, rugula and rucola; peppery green leaf eaten raw in salads or used in cooking. Baby rocket leaves are smaller and less peppery.

rolled oats flattened oat grain rolled into flakes and traditionally used for porridge. Instant oats are also available, but use traditional oats for baking.

rosewater extract made from crushed rose petals, called gulab in India; used for its aromatic quality in many sweetmeats and desserts.

saffron stigma of a member of the crocus family, available ground or in strands; imparts a yellow-orange colour to food once infused. The quality can vary greatly; the best is the most expensive spice in the world.

sauces

char siu a Chinese barbecue sauce made from sugar, water, salt, fermented soybean paste, honey, soy sauce, malt syrup and spices. It can be found at most supermarkets.

fish called naam pla on the label if it is Thai made; the Vietnamese version, nuoc naam, is almost identical. Made from pulverised salted fermented fish (most often anchovies); has a pungent smell and strong taste. There are many versions of varying intensity, so use according to your taste.

hoisin a thick, sweet and spicy Chinese barbecue sauce made from salted fermented soybeans, onions and garlic; used as a marinade or baste, or to accent stir-fries and barbecued or roasted foods. From Asian food shops and supermarkets.

oyster Asian in origin, this rich, brown sauce is made from oysters and their brine, cooked with salt and soy sauce, and thickened with starches.

plum a thick, sweet and sour dipping sauce made from plums, vinegar, sugar, chillies and spices.

soy also known as sieu; made from fermented soybeans. Several variations are available in supermarkets and Asian food stores; we use Japanese soy sauce unless indicated otherwise. *dark* deep brown, almost black in colour; rich, with a thicker consistency than other types. Pungent but not particularly salty; good for marinating. *japanese* an all-purpose low-sodium soy sauce made with more wheat content than its Chinese counterparts; fermented in barrels and aged. Possibly the best table soy and the one to choose if you only want one variety. *light* fairly thin in consistency and, while paler than the others, the saltiest tasting; used in dishes in which the natural colour of the ingredients is to be maintained. Not to be confused with salt-reduced or low-sodium soy sauces.

worcestershire thin, dark-brown spicy sauce developed by the British when in India; used as a seasoning for meat, gravies and cocktails, and as a condiment.

seafood

balmain bug also called slipper or shovelnose lobster, or southern bay lobster; crustacean, a type of crayfish. Substitute with moreton bay bugs, king prawns or scampi.

blue-eye also called deep sea trevalla or trevally and blue-eye cod; thick, moist white-fleshed fish.

clams also called vongole; we use a small ridge-shelled variety of this bivalve mollusc.

fish fillet use your favourite firm-fleshed white fish fillet.

crab meat flesh of fresh crabs; frozen uncooked flesh is also available. Use canned if neither is available.

marinara mix a mixture of uncooked, chopped seafood available from fishmarkets and fishmongers.

mussels should only be bought from a reliable fish market: they must be tightly closed when bought, indicating they are alive.

Before cooking, scrub shells with a strong brush and remove the beards; do not eat any that do not open after cooking. Varieties include black and green-lip.

octopus usually tenderised before you buy them; both octopus and squid require either long slow cooking (usually for the large molluscs) or quick cooking over high heat (usually for the small molluscs) — anything in between will make the octopus tough and rubbery.

oysters available in many varieties, including pacific, bay/blacklip, and Sydney or New Zealand rock oyster.

prawns also known as shrimp. Varieties include, school, king, royal red, Sydney harbour, tiger. Can be bought uncooked (green) or cooked, with or without shells.

salmon red-pink firm flesh with few bones; moist delicate flavour.

squid also knowns as calamari; a type of mollusc. Buy squid hoods to make preparation and cooking faster.

swordfish also called broadbill. Substitute with yellowfin or bluefin tuna or mahi mahi.

tuna reddish, firm flesh; slightly dry. Varieties include bluefin, yellowfin, skipjack or albacore; substitute with swordfish.

white fish means non-oily fish; includes bream, flathead, whiting, snapper, dhufish, redfish and ling.

sesame seeds black and white are the most common of this small oval seed, however there are also red and brown varieties. The seeds are used as an ingredient and as a condiment. Roast the seeds in a heavy-based frying pan over low heat.

shallots also called french shallots, golden shallots or eschalots. Small and elongated, with a brown-skin, they grow in tight clusters similar to garlic.

shrimp paste also called kapi, trasi and blanchan; a strong-scented, very firm preserved paste made of salted dried shrimp. Used sparingly as a flavouring in many South-East Asian soups, sauces and rice dishes. It should be chopped or sliced thinly then wrapped in foil and roasted before use.

silver beet also known as swiss chard and incorrectly, spinach; has fleshy stalks and large leaves, both of which can be prepared as for spinach.

sour cream thick, commercially-cultured sour cream with a minimum fat content of 35 per cent.

spinach also known as english spinach and incorrectly, silver beet. Baby spinach leaves are best eaten raw in salads; the larger leaves should be added last to soups, stews and stir-fries, and should be cooked until barely wilted.

star anise a dried star-shaped pod whose seeds have an astringent aniseed flavour; commonly used to flavour stocks and marinades.

sugar we use coarse, granulated table sugar, also known as crystal sugar, unless otherwise specified.

brown a soft, finely granulated sugar retaining molasses for its characteristic colour and flavour.

caster also known as superfine or finely granulated table sugar.

demerara small-grained golden-coloured crystal sugar.

icing also called confectioners' sugar or powdered sugar; pulverised granulated sugar crushed together with a small amount of cornflour.

palm also called nam tan pip, jaggery, jawa or gula melaka; made from the sap of the sugar palm tree. Light brown to black in colour and usually sold in rock-hard cakes; use with brown sugar if unavailable.

pure icing also called confectioners' sugar or powdered sugar.

sumac a purple-red, astringent spice ground from berries growing on shrubs that flourish wild around the Mediterranean; adds a tart, lemony flavour to dips and dressings and goes well with barbecued meat. Can be found in Middle Eastern food stores.

tomatoes

canned whole peeled tomatoes in natural juices; available crushed, chopped or diced, and unsalted or reduced salt. Use undrained.

cherry also called tiny tim or tom thumb tomatoes; small and round.

egg also called plum or roma, these are smallish, oval-shaped tomatoes much used in Italian cooking or salads.

grape small, long oval-shaped tomatoes with a good tomato flavour.

paste triple-concentrated tomato puree used to flavour soups, stews, sauces and casseroles.

puree canned pureed tomatoes (not tomato paste); substitute with fresh peeled and pureed tomatoes.

semi-dried partially dried tomato pieces in olive oil; softer and juicier than sun-dried, these are not a preserve thus do not keep as long as sun-dried.

sun-dried tomato pieces that have been dried with salt; this dehydrates the tomato and concentrates the flavour. We use sun-dried tomatoes packaged in oil, unless otherwise specified.

truss small vine-ripened tomatoes with vine still attached.

tarragon often called the king of herbs by the French, it is used as the essential flavouring for many of their classic sauces (béarnaise, tartare, etc). It is one of the herbs blended with parsley, chives and chervil to make fines herbes, and is the unique, immediately identified taste giving singularity to so many French egg, fish and chicken dishes.

turmeric also called kamin; is a rhizome related to galangal and ginger. Must be grated or pounded to release its acrid aroma and pungent flavour. Known for the golden colour it imparts, fresh turmeric can be substituted with the more commonly found dried powder.

vanilla

bean dried, long, thin pod from a tropical golden orchid; the minuscule black seeds inside the bean are used to impart a luscious vanilla flavour in baking and desserts.

bean paste is made from vanilla pods and contains real seeds. It is highly concentrated and 1 teaspoon replaces a whole vanilla pod without mess or fuss, as you neither have to split or scrape the pod. It can also be used instead of vanilla extract. It is found in most supermarkets in the baking section.

extract obtained from vanilla beans infused in water; a non-alcoholic version of essence.

veal

osso buco another name butchers use for veal shin, usually cut into 3cm to 5cm thick slices and used in the famous Italian slow-cooked casserole of the same name.

rack row of small chops or cutlets.

schnitzel thinly sliced steak.

vinegar

balsamic originally from Modena, Italy, there are now many balsamic vinegars on the market ranging in pungency and quality depending on how, and for how long, they have been aged. Quality can be determined up to a point by price; use the most expensive sparingly.

brown malt made from fermented malt and beech shavings.

cider made from fermented apples.

red wine made from red wine.

rice a colourless vinegar made from fermented rice and flavoured with sugar and salt. Also called seasoned rice vinegar; sherry can be substituted.

white made from distilled grain alcohol.

white wine made from white wine.

vine leaves from early spring, fresh grapevine leaves can be found in most specialist greengrocers. Alternatively, cryovac-packages containing about 60 leaves in brine can be found in Middle Eastern food shops and some delicatessens; these must be well rinsed and dried before using. Used as wrappers for a large of number of savoury fillings in Mediterranean cuisines.

walnuts as well as being a good source of fibre and healthy oils, nuts contain a range of vitamins, minerals and other beneficial plant components called phytochemicals. Each type of nut has a special make-up and walnuts contain the beneficial omega-3 fatty acids.

watercress one of the cress family, a large group of peppery greens used raw in salads, dips and sandwiches, or cooked in soups. Highly perishable, so it must be used as soon as possible after purchase.

witlof also known as belgian endive; related to and confused with chicory. A versatile vegetable, it tastes as good cooked as it does eaten raw. Grown in darkness like white asparagus to prevent it becoming green; looks somewhat like a tightly furled, cream to very light-green cigar. The leaves can be removed and used to hold a canapé filling; the whole vegetable can be opened up, stuffed then baked or casseroled; and the leaves can be tossed in a salad with other vegetables.

wombok also known as chinese cabbage, peking or napa cabbage; elongated in shape with pale green, crinkly leaves, this is the most common cabbage in South-East Asia. Can be shredded or chopped and eaten raw or braised, steamed or stir-fried.

wonton wrappers (and gow gee or spring roll pastry sheets), made of flour, egg and water, are found in the refrigerated or freezer section of Asian food shops and many supermarkets. These come in different thicknesses and shapes. Thin wrappers work best in soups, while the thicker ones are best for frying; and the choice of round or square, small or large is dependent on the recipe.

yeast (dried and fresh), a raising agent used in dough making. Granular (7g sachets) and fresh compressed (20g blocks) yeast can almost always be substituted one for the other when yeast is called for.

yogurt we use plain full-cream yogurt in our recipes unless specifically noted otherwise.

zucchini also called courgette. Harvested when young, its edible flowers can be filled with a mild cheese filling and deep-fried.

conversion chart

measures

One Australian metric measuring cup holds approximately 250ml; one Australian metric tablespoon holds 20ml; one Australian metric teaspoon holds 5ml.

The difference between one country's measuring cups and another's is within a two- or three-teaspoon variance, and will not affect your cooking results. North America, New Zealand and the United Kingdom use a 15ml tablespoon.

All cup and spoon measurements are level. The most accurate way of measuring dry ingredients is to weigh them. When measuring liquids, use a clear glass or plastic jug with the metric markings.

We use large eggs with an average weight of 60g.

dry measures

metric	imperial
15g	½oz
30g	1oz
60g	2oz
90g	3oz
125g	4oz (¼lb)
155g	5oz
185g	6oz
220g	7oz
250g	8oz (½lb)
280g	9oz
315g	10oz
345g	11oz
375g	12oz (¾lb)
410g	13oz
440g	14oz
470g	15oz
500g	16oz (1lb)
750g	24oz (1½lb)
1kg	32oz (2lb)

liquid measures

metric	imperial
30ml	1 fluid oz
60ml	2 fluid oz
100ml	3 fluid oz
125ml	4 fluid oz
150ml	5 fluid oz (¼ pint/1 gill)
190ml	6 fluid oz
250ml	8 fluid oz
300ml	10 fluid oz (½ pint)
500ml	16 fluid oz
600ml	20 fluid oz (1 pint)
1000ml (1 litre)	1¾ pints

length measures

metric	imperial
3mm	⅛in
6mm	¼in
1cm	½in
2cm	¾in
2.5cm	1in
5cm	2in
6cm	2½in
8cm	3in
10cm	4in
13cm	5in
15cm	6in
18cm	7in
20cm	8in
23cm	9in
25cm	10in
28cm	11in
30cm	12in (1ft)

oven temperatures

These oven temperatures are only a guide for conventional ovens. For fan-forced ovens, check the manufacturer's manual.

	°C (Celsius)	°F (Fahrenheit)	Gas Mark
Very slow	120	250	½
Slow	150	275-300	1-2
Moderately slow	160	325	3
Moderate	180	350-375	4-5
Moderately hot	200	400	6
Hot	220	425-450	7-8
Very hot	240	475	9